From the Library of

Julia Chistensen-Hughes

1992

THE EMPOWERED MANAGER:

POSITIVE POLITICAL

SKILLS AT WORK

PETER BLOCK

THE EMPOWERED MANAGER:

POSITIVE POLITICAL

SKILLS AT WORK

 JOSSEY-BASS PUBLISHERS

San Francisco   Oxford   1991

THE EMPOWERED MANAGER
Positive Political Skills at Work
  by Peter Block

Copyright © 1987 by: Jossey-Bass Inc., Publishers
                     350 Sansome Street
                     San Francisco, California 94104

                     Jossey-Bass Limited
                     Headington Hill Hall
                     Oxford OX3 0BW

                     Peter Block

Library of Congress Cataloging-in-Publication Data

Block, Peter.
  The empowered manager.

  (The Jossey-Bass management series)
  Bibliography: p. 209
  Includes index.
  1. Organizational behavior.   2. Organizational
effectiveness.   3. Office politics.   4. Executive
ability.   I. Title.   II. Series.
HD58.7.B58   1986   658.4   86-45619
ISBN 1-55542-019-2
ISBN 1-55542-265-9 (paperback)

Manufactured in the United States of America

The paper in this book meets the guidelines for
permanence and durability of the Committee on
Production Guidelines for Book Longevity of the
Council on Library Resources.

COVER DESIGN BY MICHAEL MARTIN

First edition
    First paperback printing: February 1991

Code 9130 (paperback)

THE JOSSEY-BASS MANAGEMENT SERIES

CONTENTS

To Peter Koestenbaum, a World Force

PREFACE TO THE PAPERBACK EDITION

The Empowered Manager was originally intended as an argument against the manipulation and negative politics that characterize large institutions. The basic premise is that negative politics is an inevitable outcome of our autocratic and patriarchal belief systems about managing organizations. The idea of empowerment evolved as an alternative to negative politics and bureaucracy.

In the time since this book was written, the concept of empowerment has exploded into the national consciousness, and concern about negative politics has faded into an interesting sidelight. And rightly so. The concern about empowerment carries with it the hope for a much more profound transformation of our institutions than did the initial concern about political skills. Empowerment promises to instill in our institutional life the same values of individual freedom, dignity, and self-governance that we readily embrace as a society. One of the failings of our democracy is that our organizations continue to be managed in an autocratic and top-down way despite our espoused belief in the fundamental value of individuals and their right to create paths of their own choosing. Many organizations have a stated vision that the employee is number one, but few have found ways to act on that belief. We as managers too often operate on the premise that the way to value employees is to take care of them, as a parent would a child. And so we have become loving parents. Benefit plans, annual increases, recognition ceremonies, employment security, company stores, and employee assistance programs are all caretaking efforts. This benevolence and paternalism, however, no longer works. It implies a promise that we cannot fulfill. In the economic environment in which we live, we can neither afford the caretaking nor guarantee the future. Also, parenting creates loyalty; it does not create a sense of responsibility and ownership. If employees believe they will be taken care of, their sense of personal responsibility and their drive to treat the organization as their own are diminished.

The promise of empowerment is that it will dramatically increase the sense of responsibility and ownership at every level of the organization, especially at the bottom where products and services are delivered and customers are served. The problem with empowerment is that it demands a radical realignment of our beliefs about control systems and the levels at which decisions are made. Every sincere effort at empowerment entails pushing governance down to lower and lower levels of the organization. The payoff is greater levels of quality and customer response. The difficulty is that it seems to require that we sell revolution to the ruling class.

It is encouraging that managers are increasingly willing to give up the control and dominance they have worked so hard to attain. They are choosing to yield sovereignty in the service of building a stronger organization with leadership valued at every level, not just at the top.

As with any idea, the popularity of empowerment carries with it the seeds of its own destruction. It risks becoming a fad and the latest cosmetic intervention that gives managers the appearance of being progressive. Here are some thoughts to increase the chances that your efforts will be successful and enduring.

BEGIN WITH YOURSELF

The universal question is, how do we empower others? How do we get other people to take responsibility for their actions and our business? The answer is, you don't empower other people. You don't give other people their freedom. You don't legislate self-esteem. You begin with yourself. You cannot give to others what you have not claimed for yourself. Claim your autonomy, your vision; declare the organization you wish to create. Live that out at every moment. Then, and only then, make it easy for others to do the same. If top management wants to create a vision or set of values for the organization, let them create it and live it out for themselves first — for two years or more. Then let them worry about how to engage others in the vision. Stop enrolling, start embodying. Enrollment is soft-core colonialism.

EMPOWERMENT IS A CHOICE, NOT A TOOL

Empowerment is not a set of techniques. Do you choose to move down the path of self-management? Is this a business strategy you believe in? If so, then over time you continually seek more and more ways to shift responsibility and control to the people doing the core work of the organization. If you fundamentally believe that leadership, direction, and control are best exercised at the top of our institutions and our society, then just say no to empowerment. Be the best parent you can be. Don't create expectations of partnership that ultimately you will not fulfill.

BEGIN THE EXPERIMENT

Stop searching and waiting for examples of where empowerment is working. All of us have to conduct the experiment in our own units and in our own lives. Knowing something is working elsewhere gives us hope, but it does not eliminate the risk or solve the problem of how we should proceed with our own revolution. We can learn from others, but at some point waiting becomes an excuse for not acting. You don't have to go to Japan to learn about quality, inventory control, continuous improvement, or serving customers. Look around inside your own organization. I do not know of one large organization, whether it is government, education, health care, or business, that is not now experimenting with empowerment strategies. The whole idea behind empowerment is that the answer lies within ourselves. Be the experimenter, the actor—not the researcher.

Finally, let me offer a comment about the response you can expect as you begin to bring empowerment ideas into your work situation. As you give your employees more and more freedom, expect a very mixed response. There is a part of each of us that does not want more autonomy, choice, or responsibility. We want to be taken care of. We like the patriarchal contract. We want our bosses to be good parents. Choosing autonomy means giving up safety. None of us gives up safety gracefully. Claiming freedom and autonomy means sacrificing innocence and security. This is the transformation we are moving through; it is difficult and demanding, and it triggers deep ambivalence. We pursue the ideas of empowerment and partnership as the means for saving and renewing ourselves and our businesses, not because our people are clamoring for them. Hopefully, over time, most of us will choose freedom and the responsibility that goes with it. The success organizations have had recently in employee involvement, self-management, quality through participation, and other similar efforts affirms this. The starting point, though, is always a willful act of leadership, a decision to engage in partnership almost independent of the responses of others or the short-term consequences.

New Providence, New Jersey   Peter Block
January 1991

ORIGINAL PREFACE

There is a quiet revolution taking place in many organizations. The source of the revolution is the growing realization that tighter controls, greater pressure, more clearly defined jobs, and tighter supervision have, in the last fifty years, run their course in their ability to give us the productivity gains we require to compete effectively in the world marketplace. Attention is shifting to the need for employees to personally take responsibility for the success of our businesses if we hope to survive and prosper.

This book presents a path to the empowerment of each employee, especially middle managers. If we wish to replace bureaucracy with entrepreneurial spirit, helplessness with empowerment, then we have to take a hard look at organizational politics. Politics is the exchange of power and so goes hand in hand with empowerment.

The cornerstone of this book is the idea that the process of organizational politics as we know it works against people's taking responsibility. We empower ourselves by discovering a positive way of being political. The line between positive and negative politics is a tightrope we have to walk. We must be powerful advocates for our units in a way that does not alienate those around and above us.

The shadow over politics as we know it is that it is synonymous with manipulation. Manipulation is so ingrained in our way of doing business that we often do not recognize it. Even if we are aware that we are engaged in a process of manipulation, we rationalize it by saying that it is a fact of life and it is the only way to get things done.

The purpose of this book is to offer hope and a path to a way of being political without being manipulative. This is a difficult undertaking because it requires changing the very meaning of the word *politics*. Politics has come to mean actions that are in the service of our own self-interest. To be political is to be self-serving on behalf of our own career and the ascendancy of the unit or function that we represent. To attack the conventional notion of politics is to strike at the heart of why we work and what kind of organization we are trying to create. The pursuit of positive politics requires us to reexamine our real self-interest, to search for alternatives to manipulation, and to renegotiate the basic contract the organization has with its employees.

Positive political skills demand that we find ways to rekindle the entrepreneurial spirit. Ways to treat all members of the organization as entrepreneurs so that employees feel that their units are their own businesses and that they, and they alone, are in the process of creating an organization of their own choosing.

The belief that it is possible for individuals to have the feeling that they are creating an organization of their own choosing is radical. The popular belief is that the direction and culture of an organization are created by the people at the top. It is the task of top management to decide what kind of organization any firm will become. This waiting for the gods to decide, and blaming the gods for not yet deciding, is in itself a symptom of the problem. To believe, fundamentally, that someone else's hands are at the controls is an expression of our dependency. This book addresses the question of who is really in charge of an organization. People at the top have tremendous impact, yet we are constantly reminded that, in very practical ways, the inmates run the prison.

The two purposes of being political in a positive way and of being entrepreneurial are the keys to our empowerment. These two ideas are the twin headlights for this book.

TO READ OR NOT TO READ

This section is designed to help you make a good decision about whether to read this book. Writing a book about organizations is not like writing an international spy thriller. In a spy thriller, you can begin by describing the fog slowly rising off the river separating two Eastern European countries. You can have a train hurtling through the night. Thick-lipped Caucasians are found in a first-class compartment, drugged, unconscious, one of them clutching a business card with a seven-legged toad embossed in green ink. A long-legged woman of indefinable background reaches quietly into her purse, her warm hand startled by the cold metal of a revolver. The train crashes, seven people are killed, and a teletype appears simultaneously in the Oval Office and in the basement of a nondescript building in Langley, Virginia. In the spy thriller, all of this happens in the first paragraph, you are hooked and off you go, knowing that you have found just the book you were looking for.

Finding a book about organizational life that has meaning for you is not so easy. You shouldn't have to read a hundred pages to decide whether you want to finish such a book. I want to tell you who this book is for and who should not read this book.

THE VIEW FROM THE BRIDGE

The Empowered Manager is written for two kinds of people: first, for executives involved in running an organization and daily struggling with how to create and leave behind an organization they personally believe in, one that expresses their deepest values about work, achievement, contribution, and the spiritual dimensions of life. Our concern at the top of an organization is not only that the organization succeed, but even more that we leave behind a legacy that ensures strength in the future. To create and leave behind a strong organization requires building a culture in which people take responsibility for themselves and the organization. In which dependency, blaming other groups, taking the safe path, seeking control for its own sake and self-serving are all minimized. That is what this book is about. Creating an entrepreneurial spirit where all members of the organization feel responsible for creating a workplace they personally believe in.

Caring about these issues means we see ourselves as forces for change and improvement. It makes us somewhat radical in the midst of a bureaucratic sea where the predominant concerns are safety, advancement, control, and the desire to hold someone else responsible for what is happening. In many ways this book is written for those with a conservative style and a radical heart. The radical heart keeps us focused on a vision of the future, on the opportunity, not the risk, of finding out what is possible. Our radical heart wishes to be practical but is willing to live on the frontier, with its dangers, and is of the belief that organizations, as the primary meeting places for human beings, have only begun to reach their potential. Our radical heart, clothed in three-piece finery, wishes not only for high overall performance but also to work in a place where the best that life has to offer is expressed. If, as a manager, these somewhat idealistic, semispiritual, softheaded ideas have meaning for you, then you have found the right book.

THE VIEW FROM THE BOILER ROOM

The book is also written for those of us who work for a living and are managers in the middle. My intent is to offer both ideas and practical ways to support the belief that we have some control over our destiny.

Working in the middle of an organization creates certain predictable dilemmas for each of us. The most difficult struggle is between serving our personal ambition to get ahead and, at the same time, doing work that has personal meaning in a way that maintains our integrity and optimism. It is easy and seductive at times to experience a sense of pessimism about the organization's ever becoming the kind of place we wish it to be. It seems often that other people are driving the business, not us, and that our survival is, in fact, in someone else's hands. How do we go about changing a culture that involves thousands of people, most of whom, from a distance, seem quite satisfied with things the way they are?

The promise of this book is that it holds an antidote to the malaise of bureaucracy. Within each of us is the ability to create an organization of our own choosing. When we believe that, it is good for us and good for the organization. That belief—that it is possible for me to create a place I believe in, even in the midst of a jungle, a desert, or the marketplace—is the entrepreneurial spirit. It is the key to being political in a positive way and to having the strength to avoid the manipulative choreography we see going on around us.

This book then is for the middle-aged and restless. Those of us who feel that most organizations are just beginning to discover what is possible. Our belief is that organizations are successful sometimes despite the way they manage themselves. That if we are going to spend the best days of our lives at work, work ought to be more than a job—and it is up to us to push the limits, regardless of our position. The desire for change, the search for better ways to handle what seem to be unsolvable problems, the wish to create something that carries our personal stamp, all grow out of feelings of dissatisfaction, restlessness, and suffering. This book is designed to scratch the itch created by both uneasiness and hope.

You, however, may view things very differently. You may feel very strongly that your organization is, in fact, currently a living example of your own deepest beliefs. You may feel that it operates very efficiently, it achieves its goals, that what is needed is more of the same. You may be an advocate for clearer goals, better structure, more willingness on the part of people to make sacrifices, and a return to a set of values that seem to have existed in the past. You may long for greater respect for authority, a greater willingness to postpone gratification, an awareness that work is work and is not meant to be the carrying vessel for life's wishes and dreams and values. You may feel that one's personal life and community life are the places for self-expression and individuality. You may argue at times that many of the jobs in today's organizations are intrinsically repetitive and hold no promise for meaning or great satisfaction. If these statements ring true and you are essentially satisfied with how your organization operates and only hope that the future is an extension of the present, then this book may not be for you.

SPECIFIC WAYS THIS BOOK CAN BE USEFUL

My intent is to offer a mix of philosophy and practicality. If you have read even this far, you have encountered most of the philosophy behind the book. Some of the more practical ways this book might be useful relate to the basic goal of developing some control over our own destiny even though we are in the middle of the organization. The book outlines specific ways to:

- Clearly see the bureaucratic pressures on us to be cautious, safe, and compliant (Chapters One and Two).

- Formulate contracts with our subordinates and bosses that encourage responsibility, self-expression, and commitment (Chapter Three).

- Create a vision of the future for our unit that embodies our deepest personal beliefs about individuals and organizations (Chapter Four).

- Develop high-integrity strategies for dealing with adversaries, fence sitters, and opponents (Chapter Five).

- Resolve within ourselves our own wish to be dependent and taken care of (Chapter Six).

- Discover the courage to do what needs to be done for ourselves and the organization (Chapter Seven).

- Develop a strategy for change that we can control (Chapter Eight).

Woven throughout the book are two additional themes:

- Ways to claim our own autonomy regardless of the expectations of others.

- Ways to develop specific methods for handling meetings, restructuring our units, managing communications, and developing other processes that align with our wish for how the organization should operate.

ACKNOWLEDGMENTS

At its best a book represents the beginning of a journey for the reader, but it represents the coming together, even closure, of a journey for the author. As in teaching, you write about those things you care about but don't quite understand, hoping that the act and stress of putting thoughts on paper for public view will give you the clarity you yearn for. Faith in this process comes from other people who have, often unknowingly, touched you along the way.

The spirit of this book was nurtured in a thousand ways by the wisdom and generosity of Peter Koestenbaum. Philosopher and friend, Peter asked me at our first meeting what my destiny was. When I couldn't answer, he asked me when I would decide. When I said I would know in a year, he said it was too long to wait. Some friend.

The thought of taking politics seriously grew out of my friendship with Larry Browning, professor at the University of Texas. Larry showed me some research he had done on organizational politics and woke me up with the thought that we could teach people to be political. This book began at that moment.

Cliff Bolster and Joel Henning, in cotraining the workshops on Positive Politics with me, contributed many of the concepts in the book. Cliff is both intellectual and pragmatic—a rare, precious combination. Joel, in addition to being as good a consultant as I know, can take a simple idea and use it in a way that gives it great depth and meaning. The two of them, along with Peter Koestenbaum, are the silent authors of this book.

I am grateful also to two top executives who paid me to consult with them and then, by their actions and our conversations, taught me what I needed to know. Noble Gividen, whom I haven't seen in fifteen years, was a district superintendent in the bureaucracy of the New York State educational system. He was politically powerful and resolutely humane, which is what this book is about. Jeff Lyle, a corporate executive, embodies the entrepreneurial spirit. He sees with brilliant clarity what the alternative to the bureaucratic mind-set looks like.

This book appeared in its first incarnation as a workshop on developing positive political skills. In addition to those mentioned above, Dominick Volini and Aubry Cramer contributed greatly in giving birth to that workshop. Dominick especially wet-nursed the workshop in its infancy through some difficult times.

The support staff at our consulting firm — Barbara Townley, Janet Newell, and Kay Callahan — contributed to this book in ways they probably didn't realize. They keep us in business by the way they deal with our clients. They represent a pure expression of placing contribution, service, and responsiveness to internal and external customers as priority number one. In writing the sections of the book about achieving greatness with users/customers, Barbara, because I primarily work with her, was one of my prime examples.

Writing a book requires a mixture of arrogance and faith. The arrogance is all mine. Neale Clapp has given unqualified support in the development of this book and my first book on consulting skills. In many ways he values what I create more than I, and for that I am forever indebted.

The final acknowledgment is to Jim Maselko. Through his deep wish to be helpful, his love of contacting others, and his unmatched skill as a trainer, Jim has created conditions that made this book possible.

New Providence, New Jersey   Peter Block
August 1986

THE AUTHOR

Peter Block has been an organization development consultant for the past twenty-five years. During this period he has been a partner, with Tony Petrella, Marvin Weisbord, and Jim Maselko, in the consulting firm of Designed Learning, Inc., in Plainfield, New Jersey.

In 1981, Block wrote *Flawless Consulting*, a book about how to function in a staff capacity with maximum impact and leverage. *Flawless Consulting* became the basis for Designed Learning's staff consulting skills workshops, which are designed for engineers, systems people, personnel professionals, and others in the staff role. Since 1981, close to 15,000 people have attended the workshop.

Since the mid sixties, Block's work has been to foster the idea of empowerment and the hope it offers to people in organizations. *The Empowered Manager* attempts to integrate and crystallize that effort. Designed Learning currently offers a workshop based on the concepts presented in this book. For information on the workshop or consulting efforts to implement these ideas contact Designed Learning in Plainfield, New Jersey.

Block received his bachelor's degree in industrial management from the University of Kansas and his master's degree in organizational behavior from Yale University. He is a board member of the Association for Quality and Participation; a member of the advisory board of Reimer & Koger, an investment counseling firm; and a member of the Instructional Systems Association.

Peter and his wife, Barbara, have four grown children and live in Mystic, Connecticut.

THE EMPOWERED MANAGER:

POSITIVE POLITICAL

SKILLS AT WORK

THE DILEMMAS OF MANAGERS

IN THE MIDDLE

One of the forces drawing us toward empowering people in the middle and lower levels of organizations is the fact that bigger is no longer better. Most large companies are reducing the number of employees as fast as they can, often eliminating whole layers of management in their attempt to be more efficient. This effort at pushing responsibility downward is a direct assault on the bureaucratic methods and mind-set that characterize life in most organizations.

Reducing bureaucracy requires more than simply reducing jobs and becoming more lean. It requires an attitude shift on the part of people in the middle toward feeling empowered to do what is truly best for themselves and for the business. At the deepest level, the enemy of high-performing systems is the feeling of helplessness that so many of us in organizations seem to experience. We are caught between the need for managers to stand firm for their beliefs and yet realize there are always people who have power over us and can blow out our candle without even taking a deep breath.

The simplest way to capture the dilemma this book addresses is by telling you the story of Allan. Allan is a top executive who for me symbolizes both the deepest hope we have for what organizations can become and also the harsh reality of what each of us confronts on almost a daily basis.

When I first met Allan five years ago, he was a group product manager for a large health care company. He was in his mid thirties and responsible for the marketing of a line of health care products. Allan was bright, knew his business, and was very aggressive in both his approach to the marketplace and his approach to the people around him. He was constantly pushing for changes in the way the company did business. His product line consistently met its financial goals, but his rather impatient, task-oriented, at times judgmental style of operating began to get him in hot water. He was told that he needed to become more of a team player, was pushing against the structure a little too vigorously, and if he could just ease up a bit, he would have a fine career with this company.

This dialogue finally reached a point at which a promotion was withheld because of the feathers he was ruffling. At the same time a proposal Allan had made to bring a new product to market was put on a back burner. In the face of these two setbacks, Allan bolted. He initiated a job search for an organization that would value his entrepreneurial energy and give him the opportunity to initiate a truly successful new venture. His search uncovered a pharmaceutical company that was looking to move into new businesses. The head of the company offered Allan the opportunity to study the feasibility of this new business, and if the company decided to move ahead, Allan would run the new division. Allan took the job, leaving the health care company with some bitterness and the belief that its bureaucratic mentality was the problem.

The pharmaceutical company decided to go ahead with the new venture and Allan was made president of the new division. Allan was determined to build an entrepreneurial organization in the midst of the conservative pharmaceutical company that he recently joined. His goal was to hire people who were willing to take the risk of an entrepreneurial venture and to create a culture that valued initiative, absolute honesty, and achievement. Every organization says it values these qualities, but Allan wanted to make these entrepreneurial ideals a day-to-day reality.

Over the next four years Allan became first a client and eventually a friend of mine. With my role as a kind of social architect, we devised as many ways as we could think of to structure the organization to encourage people to feel empowered and responsible for the success of the business. A reward system was established whereby a significant part of each person's salary was based on the profitability of the division. Allan pushed decision making to the lowest level. The staff made all its own decisions about equipment, structure, working procedures, and performance criteria and evaluation. Perquisites such as office size and decor, parking spaces, vacation time, eating areas, and the like were the same for everyone in the company, including Allan. Every action and policy was designed to create an alternative to the cautious, bureaucratic, and political environments in which everyone had previously worked.

Despite some ups and downs, the strategy essentially worked. The division became profitable after two years and passed $40 million in sales in the third year. Needless to say, Allan was an ideal client for me and over the years actually became a role model for many of the ideas that this book expresses. The experience with Allan gave me faith that it is indeed possible to create an organization of our own choosing even though we are surrounded by an organization steeped in conservative tradition. Throughout this process, Allan was forced to constantly defend and explain the way he was managing his division. The more successful the division became, the more attention it got, the greater the discomfort his practices created among other executives in the company. But the bottom line was that he had created an entrepreneurial unit and even though the number of people in the division was growing rapidly, the spirit survived.

How I wish that the story ended here, but it doesn't. As I was completing this book about people's taking responsibility, being political in a positive way, and not getting caught up in the negative politics surrounding them, I got a phone call from Allan.

He had just had a meeting with his boss, an executive vice president of the parent company, and been asked to resign. He was told that top management had been growing increasingly uncomfortable with him, that the chemistry wasn't good, and that top management had decided to replace Allan with one of his subordinates. In the previous six months, Allan's division had been under increasing scrutiny and Allan had evidently responded with considerable aggression, some anger, and probably more than a little arrogance—all qualities we tend to associate with entrepreneurial, individualistic people. Allan took his exit quite well. He was getting weary of having to defend his actions and, in fact, took more pleasure in creating a business than in maintaining it.

I, however, took his demise quite poorly. How could he do this to me? Here I was writing a book using him as one of my positive role models and he goes and gets himself fired. The least he could have done was wait until the book was published before he crashed and burned. I did not express my self-centered concerns to Allan on the phone at that time. I expressed my support and wished him well, knowing that he would land on his feet, which he has. Two months later, he finalized a deal whereby he would start up another health care company for some venture capitalists and he would have total control over the business and no accountability other than profitability.

His problem is solved, but the dilemma facing the focus of this book is not. Allan's dilemma in the pharmaceutical company is the same dilemma that faces each person who manages a group as part of a larger organization. There is a bit of Allan in each of us. On the one hand we have strong beliefs about how we want to manage our own unit; on the other hand we have people above and around us who wish us to be much more traditional and cautious. They counsel us to be patient, to be sensitive to the wishes of people in power, and they remind us that change is a slow and evolutionary process. The meaning of Allan's story is that it speaks to a hope and a fear in each of us. The hope is that we can totally be ourselves and act according to our own beliefs and wants and still be accepted. We have hopes to improve our organization and make it a place where people take responsibility, where reasonable risks are valued, where getting results is more important than pleasing others, where substance is more important than form. At the same time, we fear that this is not possible — that Allan's ending will be our ending, except that we will not land on our feet. We will land on our knees and stay there. Our primitive fear in organizations is that if we stand up, we will be shot. This book is about standing up without getting shot.

The goal of this book is to present a way of being political that balances the hope for transforming organizations with the risks in attempting change, in a realistic and helpful way. Making changes in organizations in a way that maintains support from those around us is what political skill is all about. The first step in taking the best of what Allan offers, his courage, his vision, his willingness to risk, without stepping on the rake of our own arrogance and aggression, is to begin a dialogue about politics itself.

There is no more engaging and volatile aspect of work life than the dimension of organizational politics. In most places, people are not comfortable discussing politics openly. Politics in organizations is like sex was in the 1950s — we knew it was going on, but nobody would really tell us about it. The same with politics — we know it is woven in the fabric of our work, but to get reliable information about it is next to impossible. In fact, the first rule of politics is that nobody will tell you the rules. This is changing somewhat in the increasingly large number of available books that tell us how to work the politics of our organization to our advantage. But even in these books, politics is basically a negative process. If I told you you were a very political person, you would take it either as an insult or at best as a mixed blessing.

The breeding ground for politics as we know it is the bureaucratic mind-set that pervades life in organizations. The essence of a bureaucratic way of doing business is the choice for safety, caution, and control. In our search for positive political acts we are forced to confront those forces in the organization that support bureaucracy and make the internal entrepreneur a rare species.

This book offers an antidote to the bureaucratic mentality that is bred in organizations. Bureaucracy is a state of mind and exists regardless of the size of the organization. The core of the bureaucratic mind-set is not to take responsibility for what is happening. Other people are the problem. Bureaucracy is elusive because we always think it characterizes someone else, never ourselves. Thus, efforts to improve our organization too often involve discussion of people outside the room that we are in at the moment.

This attitude that it is not my fault is the essence of bureaucracy. The alternative to the bureaucrat is the entrepreneur. The entrepreneur is the folk hero, the cowboy, the Lindbergh of organizational life. Most organizations were begun by someone who was willing to bet the farm, but as an organization grows and succeeds, it also creates the conditions for its own destruction. The need for bigness, economy of scale, coordination, and structure all work against the spirit of risk and responsibility that breathed life into the firm in the first place.

Reawakening the original spirit means we have to confront the issue of our own autonomy. To pursue autonomy in the midst of a dependency-creating culture is an entrepreneurial act. This book is, in fact, written for those who think of themselves as being in the middle and who wish to create a culture and spirit of their own choosing.

Part One presents ways of creating an *environment* and culture that support empowerment. Part Two discusses what we as *individuals* can do to reduce our feeling of futility and make our workplace an expression of our deepest values.

PERSONAL CHOICES THAT SHAPE

THE WORK ENVIRONMENT

In being political we walk the tightrope between advocating our own position and yet not increasing resistance against us by our actions. The path we take is a mixture of two forces: the individual choices we make in adapting to our environment and the nature of the norms and values of the organization we find ourselves imbedded in. Let's begin with the choices we have as individuals.

As managers, our fundamental purpose is to build a department and organization that we are proud of. Our unit in many ways becomes a living monument to our deepest beliefs in what is possible at work. We strive to create both a high-performing unit and one that treats its own members and its customers well. Each time we act as a living example of how we want the whole organization to operate, it is a positive political act.

Organizations have limited resources, limited budgets, limited people, and a limited number of actions they can attempt. We want at least our fair share of those resources. Therefore, the methods we use in reaching for those resources are at the heart of politics.

If we get what we want but do it in a way that we do not feel good about, we are in a quandary. We have achieved our short-term goal but acted in a way that is not an example of how we want the rest of the organization to operate. This dilemma became very vivid to me in a lunch meeting I had with the president of a major chemicals company. We had talked at length about his vision of greatness, the human values he wished to see expressed in his organization, and the fact that those values were not a dominant part of the culture of his company. He had discussed the difficulties he had with his boss and how careful the president had to be around his boss, who was chairman of the company. The president also talked about his wish to become chairman some day and his doubts that this would happen. After listening to him talk about these very personal matters with me, a relative stranger who would be deemed rather softheaded in his circles, I asked him why he was even having this conversation. His company was making record profits; as president, he was sitting on top of the heap. Why was he looking for help? His answer was that two of his children had graduated from college in recent years. As each graduated and began looking for a job in industry, the president realized that his company did not provide the kind of environment he wanted his own children to work in. The company was very competitive, people were valued about sixth on the scale of importance, and he wished his own children would find a different culture in which to start their careers. A powerful statement from one at the top.

This man, his name is Phil, would have to be judged politically sophisticated along any criterion, having reached the top of a major U.S. corporation. Yet having reached his goal was not enough. The way that he got there and the kind of organization that he helped create in the process made a difference. He played a game well, even though he had doubts about the game he was playing. This is not just Phil's problem. Phil is a thoughtful person, and in a way, he speaks for each of us.

Having grown up in a traditional, hierarchical organization with patriarchal values, too many of us believe that in order to manage the politics of our situation, we must become good at

- manipulating situations and, at times, people,

- managing information and plans carefully to our own advantage,

- invoking the names of high-level people when seeking support for our projects,

- becoming calculating in the way we manage relationships,

- paying great attention to what the people above us want from us,

- living with the belief that in order to get ahead, we must be cautious in telling the truth.

These are elements of what is generally called playing the game. Playing the game well is what we mean when we talk about conventional corporate politics. Unfortunately, most popular books on politics are quite grim and pessimistic in their outlook. They teach us how to win through intimidation, how to win at office politics, how to dress for success, how to move up fast and pull our own strings. The problem is that getting better at maneuvering-type politics is not a very satisfying solution, even though it works. Why get better at a bad game? Our purpose is to create a good game. The good game involves acting as an entrepreneur for our unit and being political in the best sense of the word. Being political as an act of service, contribution, and creation.

One of the reasons that conventional politics is so common is that it's hard for us to see clearly what options we have.

NOW YOU SEE IT, NOW YOU DON'T

There is a unique quality to organizational politics that makes it an elusive topic. This quality is self-blindness: It is easy to see political acts in others but almost impossible to see them in ourselves. When *you* avoid sensitive issues, curry favor with powerful people, and shade the truth for the sake of your own self-interest, I notice it quite easily. When *I* do those things myself, the situation takes on a whole different flavor. In my own mind, I am simply adapting to the practical realities of the world and taking those actions needed to get support for my projects. I have never heard anyone acknowledge that "Yes, I do engage in acts of manipulation and deception and interpersonal arm wrestling. I do it as a planned strategy for achieving my goals, and I think it is the most effective way to operate." Instead, we rationalize our actions by explaining that we took them only once, that they were caused by others, and that what we did really was not manipulation.

Another expression of the self-blindness quality of politics is that we see clearly the political moves of those above us in the organization but operate in a fog when trying to see the political activity of those who work for us. My subordinates are all working hard trying to do a good job. Once in a while I see them take a subtle shot at each other and once in a while they talk to me about their peers in an undercutting way, but to me, the boss, this activity seems rather minor and inconsequential to the kind of organization I am working to create.

Now, when we talk about our superiors, that is a different story. Each of us can give detailed accounts of the melodrama of aggression and irrationality that exists above us in the organization.

Our acute awareness of the political moves of others, especially those above us in the organization, is in part an expression of our dependency. I fear those that I feel dependent upon. If you have power over me it makes me cautious and watchful. I watch your reactions; I learn all I can about how you operate, what you like and don't like, how to present myself in a winning way.

Within my own department, it is a different story. Looking down I see people who are dependent on me, who worry about pleasing me, so there is less to be fearful of, and the subtle moves among my subordinates are not something I need to pay close attention to.

CHOOSING AN ENTREPRENEURIAL PATH

This unbalanced way of viewing the political dynamics and possibilities around us stems from the experience of being in a low-power or less-power position. Since we all have bosses, we experience ourselves as reacting to people and events outside ourselves. This results in a reluctance to take full responsibility for our own actions and for the organization that we are in the process of creating. Even in the face of the reality that there is always someone in the organization who has power over us, it is important to realize that we still have choices. At any point in time, how we choose drives us in either an entrepreneurial or a bureaucratic direction. The connection being made is that an entrepreneurial mind-set is equivalent to being political in a positive way. A bureaucratic mind-set is equivalent to acting out negative politics as we know it. The fundamental choices we make are these:

We choose between Maintenance and Greatness.

We choose between Caution and Courage.

We choose between Dependency and Autonomy.

These choices define the tightrope we walk.

MAINTENANCE VERSUS GREATNESS

When we choose maintenance, we are trying to hold on to what we have created or inherited. Our wish is to not lose ground. A bureaucratic culture constantly drives us toward a maintenance mentality. To maintain what we have is to be preoccupied with safety. The popular desire to keep moving up in the organization carries with it the fear of falling. The bureaucratic belief is that we will move ahead in the organization by not making any mistakes. The common feeling is that mistakes are punished much more vigorously than achievements are rewarded. It seems that the higher in the organization we go, the more dominant this feeling becomes. We might have the illusion that as we move up the ladder, confidence will build and risk taking will increase. But the opposite often occurs. The higher we go, the greater the wish for safety and the desire to hold on to what we have. The greater the fall, the greater the tragedy and the greater the wish for maintenance.

When you ask individuals how they are doing, the response is "Not bad." This is the top of the scale; it is as good as it gets. For things to be not bad. The possibility that things could be good, great, or exciting is not even in the cards.

The choice for maintenance is the choice to be led by others. The bureaucratic belief in policies and procedures is the source of our security. Holding onto what we have causes us to stay away from the frontier and to surround ourselves with corporate insulation of structure and predictability.

The alternative to a maintenance mentality is to choose some form of greatness. *Greatness* is a difficult word to come to terms with. It implies a degree of arrogance and immortality that many of us feel is inappropriate in the context of our work. When managers are asked what form of greatness they wish for their unit, the common response is "Give me a break. I'm just trying to make a living and keep my head above water, waiting for the motorboat to come by." We tend to believe that greatness is reserved for the Albert Schweitzers, Bishop Tutus, and Mickey Mantles of the world. We want to substitute other words for greatness.

People say, "Can't we use the word *improvement* instead of *greatness*?" Our reluctance to choose greatness is another expression of our caution and perhaps pessimism regarding what is possible at work. Despite the caution, many managers have in fact chosen greatness and are committing their energy to making it a reality. Many managers are deeply committed to creating an organization that is different from the one that they grew up in. What is appealing about Allan, the president of the new division discussed in the introduction, is that he had no other goal than to create a business that did not operate like the consumer products company in which he spent the first fifteen years of his career. He wanted to create an entrepreneurial organization and tried to express that in areas such as office size and decor, who was invited to meetings of the management committee, the decisions that secretaries made, the compensation plan for all employees, and in a hundred other symbolic ways that communicated that his organization was unique and striving for something beyond what its members had experienced before. The fact that Allan ultimately ran into a wall doesn't diminish the meaning of his choice for greatness.

The immense popularity of Peters and Waterman's *In Search of Excellence*[1] is an expression of the desire to find an alternative to traditional organization life. The choice for greatness is the commitment to operate and achieve in a unique way. It is a risky choice because we know that even if we choose greatness, we may never achieve it. Choosing a unique path in the midst of a large bureaucracy always feels like a dangerous path. And this is not just a feeling; it is dangerous. But that is what gives the choice for greatness meaning. Following a path of high risk, where the outcome is in doubt, is the essence of the entrepreneurial spirit. Allan's decision to provide equal office space for professionals at all levels, to open management committee meetings to all employees, to allow secretaries to make all of their own equipment purchase decisions, and to suggest that employee compensation should in large part be determined by the profitability of the company were all radical acts.

---

[1] T. J. Peters and R. H. Waterman, *In Search of Excellence: Lessons from America's Best Run Companies* (New York: Harper & Row, 1982).

He spent half of his time negotiating with the parent company for these kinds of changes, and he lost many of the battles.

Allan, despite his aggression and arrogance, chose greatness, and whether or not his organization could successfully create a unique pocket of entrepreneurship in the midst of a bureaucracy in some ways does not make any difference. It is the commitment that is significant. Each of us has the opportunity to make a commitment to greatness in the context of his or her own job. To be entrepreneurial and to be political in a positive way requires as a first step the choice between maintaining what we have and choosing some form of greatness.

CAUTION VERSUS COURAGE

The second fundamental choice we make in creating the entrepreneurial spirit is between caution and courage. Most of the external messages we receive seem to demand caution. There are the highly institutionalized efforts that give us the feeling that we are constantly being watched and evaluated. Performance reviews are the annual events that remind us that a judge is in the wings making sure that we follow the common path. We have all had performance reviews early in our career when our supervisor told us that for our own good we needed to develop more maturity and political sensitivity. The feedback we receive in performance reviews is couched in the words "We, the management of the company, have agreed that the following are areas you need to work on for your own development." The words "We, the management" give us the image that sitting behind our supervisor are hundreds of other managers in the company, all of one mind about what we, the employees, need to work on. Who can help but feel cautious in the face of this powerful consensus?

Hundreds of other signals drive us toward caution. In many companies the process of giving presentations to management carries the message to be careful. It is common to go through a number of dry runs before presenting a project review to a management group. We produce perfect overhead transparencies summarizing the major points, all perfectly produced. After the perfect overhead transparencies are developed, we then rehearse the presentation several times. By the time the actual presentation rolls around, we almost lose interest in the subject matter. The underlying message from this process of review and control is that we have to be careful. Presentations are the one or two occasions during the year when we get exposure to top-level people, and we don't want to make a mistake.

Performance reviews and presentations to management symbolize the pressure to be careful. They are merely two of a hundred events that drive us toward caution.

The alternative to caution is to choose courage. In our culture, moving forward and creating an organization we believe in always requires an act of courage. The courage comes in the form of a series of small steps, taken mostly in private two-person conversations in which we are the only one keenly aware of the risk we are taking. To act courageously is to follow an unpopular path. To confront an issue when others are acting as if there is no issue; to say that a meeting is not going well when everyone else seems totally satisfied. This is not a bells and whistles kind of courage. It is not the courage of theater, where the sides are clearly drawn and we stand up for truth and justice. When truth, justice, and morality are at stake, standing up is simpler because we know that we have God on our side. Organizational courage is required when the sides are somewhat murky, when the issue in and of itself is less than monumental, and when we feel that top management is in fact not on our side. The choice for self-assertion and risk is the only antidote for caution and the choice to maintain what we have inherited. The hard part is to be able to tell the difference between courage and suicide, and that is what this book is about.

The third and final choice we make is between dependency and autonomy. We are told the organization values autonomy and are treated like children. This double message from those above us may be a gift in disguise. If there are messages about standing up (autonomy) and bending over (dependency) that conflict with each other, this gives us the freedom to make our own choice. Autonomy is the attitude that my actions are my own choices and the organization I am a part of is in many ways my own creation. It puts us in the center and in charge of what is happening at the moment. We are the cause, not the effect.

It is difficult to maintain this attitude in the middle of a pyramid containing many levels of management, whose offices get larger as one moves up the ladder. The fundamental vulnerability in the way most large organizations are managed is the pervasive feeling of dependency that is engendered. When we feel dependent we are waiting for something above or below us to give us direction.

We hear people constantly call for strong leadership. Everyone is waiting for top management to get its act together. "When is top management going to give vision and direction to this organization?" We focus a great deal on supervisory style and say with certainty that the supervisor sets the tone for how other people behave. We secretly wish that we were working for Lee Iacocca, for he is a man of vision and strong leadership. We point to the need for a strong culture and wish that Tom Peters were sitting with our boss right now making the case for managing by walking around and demanding that we get close to the customer. When things go wrong we blame it on the "culture." All of these wishes for changes above us are an expression of our dependency. They all imply that until something above me changes, don't expect me to operate much differently. All of this looking upward and preoccupation with the people in power is an expression of our dependency.

It is comforting to be led. It feels safe and implies a promise that if we follow, our future will be assured. The choice for dependency is a step into the mainstream along a conventional path. As organizations get larger, the need for coordination and control and consistency increases, and the unintended consequence is the proliferation of a dependent mind-set. The price we pay for dependency is our own sense of helplessness. Helplessness and waiting for clear instructions before acting are the opposite of the entrepreneurial spirit. Each of us has to decide — whose organization is this? If I want to feel a sense of ownership in this organization where I spend the best days of my life, I must confront my own wish for dependency and move in the direction of autonomy. Knowing all along the way that I do have a choice and that, in fact, dependency may be the safer path.

When we choose autonomy we realize that there is nothing to wait for. We do not require anything from those above us to create a unit or department of our own choosing. An autonomous or entrepreneurial mind-set means that I must commit myself to managing my unit in a way that makes sense to me and that the weight of the organization is on my shoulders. It is heavy but it is also liberating.

I can now get on with the business of serving my users and customers and managing a unit in a way that expresses my own personal values about how organizations should work. If the people in power above do not like what I am doing, let them stop me. Better to proceed than to wait for direction. Better to ask forgiveness than permission. Better to be seen as stubborn than incompetent. This is the high-risk, high-anxiety, high-integrity choice each of us has to make When we choose the path of high resistance and decide that the future of our own unit is in our own hands, it is good for the organization as a whole.

Even though we may wish constantly to choose greatness, courage, and autonomy, there are times when we feel this is simply not possible or realistic. Knowing when to risk and when to lie low is the tightrope we walk, especially as middle managers. The difficult thing about being in the middle of an organization is that the amount of power we have is often ambiguous. At the bottom of the organization there is nothing ambiguous about the amount of direct power we have. The answer is none. At the top of the organization, our power is also clear. It is absolute (at least in theory). Granted, people at the bottom have more power than they realize, and people at the top have less power than is attributed to them. But the basic rights of these two levels are comparatively clear. Working in the middle levels as a supervisor or manager is more like never-never land.

There are times when choosing maintenance, caution, and dependency is realistic and in our best interest:

New and unknowing. When we are new in a job or the work is changing in a direction in which we have little knowledge, it makes sense to lie low for a while (six months at most). With a new position or a new boss, it takes a while to build enough trust in the relationships around us to withstand the pressure of changes and risks we wish to take. It also takes a while for us to know just where to focus our entrepreneurial energy.

Survival is at stake. When our business is struggling and we are worrying about making it through the quarter or the year, all of our conservative juices are triggered. All of our instincts tell us to stay with what we know and to keep life simple. Unfortunately, we may be in a survival mode simply because we have been too cautious in the past, so if we continue to do more of what we have traditionally done, we will make things worse. The sad thing about dealing with failing organizations is that in the anxiety of their struggle, they are least able to accept help or really face up to the cause of their problems or take the risks needed to turn the situation around.

Following periods of risk and expansion. There is a rhythm to our ability to act with courage and autonomy and our need to rest and consolidate. Periods of strong advocacy and adventure need to be followed by periods (not too long) of caution and dependency.

Zero trust environment. Positive political acts require a certain level of trust in our environment and in the people we work with. The worst case occurs when we feel that our boss is our adversary. Maintaining what we have, being cautious in what we say and do, and letting those above us think that they own us are survival strategies in a desert of support. If the condition persists, we have to ask ourselves why we stay in the situation; and "to pay the mortgage" is not an adequate answer.

ORIGINS OF THE

BUREAUCRATIC MENTALITY

In addition to the individual choice we make for caution or courage at a specific moment, we are impacted by both norms and practices of our organization and the set of beliefs and values we bring to the job. We need to understand the nature of the tightrope we are on before we can begin to walk it. The next two chapters describe what drives us toward a bureaucratic, negatively political journey and outline what the alternative, more entrepreneurial and positive path would be. Four elements are critical in understanding organizational politics: the contract between the individual and the organization, how each of us defines his or her self-interest, the tactics we use in generating support for our activities, and the basic autonomy or dependency that each cycle fosters. These elements form a self-reinforcing cycle that results in either an entrepreneurial or a bureaucratic way of operating (Figure 1).

Ultimately, it is by moving toward the entrepreneurial cycle that our approach toward positive politics becomes realized. After exploring the bureaucratic and entrepreneurial cycles, we can look at ways in which we, as managers, can be advocates for our function in a positive way.

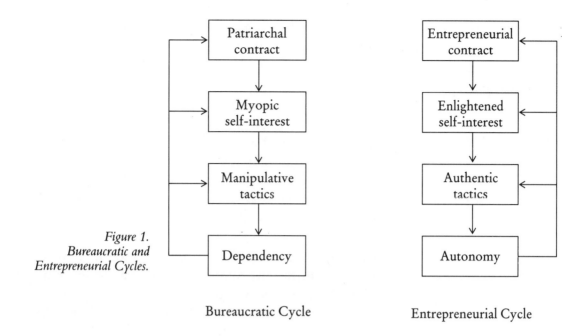

Figure 1.
Bureaucratic and
Entrepreneurial Cycles.

Bureaucratic Cycle   Entrepreneurial Cycle

THE BUREAUCRATIC CYCLE

In many ways, organizations unintentionally encourage people to choose to maintain what they have, to be cautious
and dependent. Every organization was started by someone
who bet the farm to offer a new product or service — an entrepreneur. It doesn't matter whether the organization was a
hospital, a government agency, a church, or a business. The
organization you are a part of now was started by an instinctive
act of greatness, courage, and autonomy. As the organization
grew, it decided that more structure and control were needed.
Roles and responsibilities needed clearer definition. People
demanded consistency and uniform treatment. The second
or third generation of "professional management" was
brought in, and the seeds of bureaucracy were sown. How
does the spirit that creates an organization get diluted? A self-
reinforcing cycle gets triggered with size and success and

results in encouraging bureaucratic and political behavior. To create an entrepreneurial approach, we must break this cycle.

The bureaucratic cycle has four parts:

PART ONE: THE PATRIARCHAL CONTRACT.[2]   The cycle begins with the basic contract between the organization and the employee. The traditional contract is patriarchal in its emphasis on a top-down, high-control orientation. It stems from the success that the military and the church have historically had with centralized control and clarity of roles, levels of authority, and the need for discipline and self-control.

PART TWO: MYOPIC SELF-INTEREST.   Success is defined in most traditional organizations as moving up the ladder, gaining more and more authority and responsibility, and being rewarded financially for the effort. People define self-interest in terms of personal rewards rather than in terms of service and contribution to others. Because the patriarchal contract gives such emphasis to control and authority, new employees soon shift their focus from doing meaningful work to moving up the hierarchy. Granted, we each enter an organization with strong instincts toward upward mobility, but the culture's own authority-oriented value system greatly intensifies those ambitions. A hierarchical power-oriented culture breeds hierarchical power-oriented people.

PART THREE: MANIPULATIVE TACTICS.   An autocratic culture and personal ambition conspire to support behavior that is strategic, cautious, and indirect — in other words, manipulative. Manipulation is controlling people without letting them know you are doing so. Manipulation is tolerated in most organizations and often implicitly admired. Traditional politics is the art of manipulation. The common belief is that we have to be

---

[2] The concept of the patriarchal contract is taken from David McClelland, *Power — The Inner Experience* (New York: Irvington, 1979), pp. 183–184.

manipulative to get to the top. The only people who deny this are the people at the top. When they deny it, we wonder if they are really being honest with us. We think they are being manipulative even in the act of claiming that their success was not based on politics.

PART FOUR: DEPENDENCY.   The patriarchal contract, the narrow definition of self-interest, and the manipulative strategies feed and reinforce each other in a way that nurtures a dependent mentality. The belief that our survival is in someone else's hands is in part a consequence of the first three parts of the bureaucratic cycle. Our initial willingness to be dependent also helps to create the cycle. After twelve or so years of school systems and family that treat us fundamentally as children, we are conditioned for more of the same. We may not wish to be dependent, but dangle a reward system in front of our eyes and we are ripe for the picking.

THE ENTREPRENEURIAL CYCLE

The alternative to the bureaucratic cycle is the entrepreneurial cycle. Positive political skills involve acting with autonomy and compassion in service of a vision, which is very aligned with the entrepreneurial spirit. The original meaning of politics was to act in service of society. Politics was a high form of public service. Of late it has lost its dignity and been reinterpreted to mean acting in service of self. Politics has become self-serving; thus, the negative connotation. Positive politics is acting to best serve our customers, inside the company and out, letting our actions be an antidote to the cautious, dependent, bureaucratic behavior we are too familiar with. Becoming positively political is to act as if the whole organization we are a part of is in fact our own. And if it is my business, then I will be the one to decide what it will become. This mind-set is at the heart of the entrepreneurial behavior in our organizations, and it drives our political behavior toward service and contribution. Our goal is to have all members believe and act like this is their organization and to take personal responsibility for how it operates. This begins to happen when we move toward an entrepreneurial cycle.

PART ONE: THE ENTREPRENEURIAL CONTRACT. The entrepreneurial cycle begins with a contract that is based on the belief that the most trustworthy source of authority comes from within the person. The primary task of supervision is to help people trust their own instincts and take responsibility for the success of the business. The contract demands that people make a serious commitment to the organization but do so because they want to, not because they have to. The expectation is that people at each level will treat the business as their own.

PART TWO: ENLIGHTENED SELF-INTEREST. Rather than defining success as moving up in the organization, we define success in terms of contribution and service to customers and other departments. What we offer people as rewards are jobs that have meaning, the opportunity to learn and create something special, and the chance to grow in a business through their own efforts. Advancement and pay are still important but are given a secondary focus.

PART THREE: AUTHENTIC TACTICS. An entrepreneurial contract encourages us to be direct and authentic in our management style. If we begin to believe that it is our business, then we will feel empowered to act on our own values. For most of us this will mean letting people know where they stand, sharing as much information as possible, sharing control, and taking reasonable risks. These are the kinds of tactics that minimize the belief that we have to be calculating and controlled in order to move up the ladder. The good news is that it makes sense; the bad news is that much of our experience tells us that it takes courage.

PART FOUR: AUTONOMY. The entrepreneurial contract and a service-oriented definition of self-interest support each of us in claiming our own autonomy. Autonomy reduces the need for us to give so much attention and power to those above us. It reduces our fear of being shot and demands that we own our own actions. Each of us will always at times continue to choose caution, maintenance, and dependency, but the basic beliefs of the organization will operate to support greatness, courage, and independence.

THE PATRIARCHAL CONTRACT: ORIGIN OF DEPENDENCY

To understand the underlying forces that support traditional political approaches, we need to take a closer look at each part of the bureaucratic and entrepreneurial cycles. Both begin with a basic contract.

The bureaucratic cycle begins with a patriarchal contract. When we sign on with an organization, we agree to four core elements that guide our behavior:

- submission to authority,

- denial of self-expression,

- sacrifice for unnamed future rewards,

- belief that the above are just.

SUBMISSION TO AUTHORITY. When we enter the door, the first thing we are told is whom we report to. Everybody in the organization has a boss. It was always amazing to me when AT&T was one organization with over one million employees that everybody in the organization knew who his or her supervisor was and had a boss. There must have been hundreds of people whose only job was to make sure that everybody had a boss. The belief was that if one person among that million employees did not have a boss, the whole system would somehow be undermined.

A basic tenet of most organizations is that the lines of authority need to be clear and understood and that we must submit to authority. The authority relationship must remain unquestioned, and if a person does not submit to authority, he is labeled with the ultimate accusation — disloyalty.

Testing or confusing the authority relationship puts us on tenuous ground. Every organization has what it calls an "open door" policy, which implies that people can always go around their boss and talk to anybody that they wish. The reality is that the doors are open but nobody ever walks through them. We all know that the authority relationship with our boss can be tampered with only in extreme or accidental circumstances.

In some organizational forms, such as a matrix, the lines of authority are not clear. One person may report to two bosses. One boss may be in charge of a functional specialty, such as engineering or finance, and the other boss may be in charge of a major project and be called a project manager. This creates tremendous stress in people, and the constant complaint is "I don't know who my boss is." If a person has two or three bosses, then the feeling is that the working situation is almost untenable.

We constantly hear project managers in a matrix system complain about the fact that there are no direct lines of authority and they need something from people that they have no control over. Such complaints communicate the idea that this is a major organizational flaw — that the clear authority, one-boss relationship is missing.

The key element of the part of the contract that requires our submission to authority is the word *submission*. When we demand that people submit to authority, we are saying that the fundamental and most trustworthy source of knowledge is outside of oneself. There is wisdom external to ourselves that needs to be revered and respected. It is this reverence of the external authority in the organization that leads to our very strong feeling of dependency and our wish for approval. The higher the authority, the greater we wish the authority's approval. As an employee, there is a payoff for us in the emphasis on submitting to authority. It is our ultimate excuse when something goes wrong; what better person to blame than our own supervisor. We spend an incredible amount of time focusing on and talking about our supervisor. We have a deep wish for a perfect supervisor, just as we had a deep wish for a perfect parent. Ultimately, our supervisor falls short of our hopes and expectations, and we are grateful that our supervisor, or manager, or top managers are less than perfect because it absolves us of responsibility. Our willingness to submit to authority rewards us by letting us off the hook. It means that when something goes wrong, it's not our fault. It was either top management's fault for taking us in that direction or, if we are a manager, it is our subordinate's fault for not understanding our instructions and not being properly motivated.

The price the organization pays for giving such emphasis to authority is the feeling of helplessness it creates. If it's not my fault, I can't fix it. This is the collusion between the management and the people working for them. Managers take comfort in the fact that there are people under their control who are forced to submit to their wishes, and this gives them the illusion of power and influence.

Subordinates take comfort in the fact that when things go wrong, it is not their fault; and the fact that they pay for this comfort with their own helplessness is a small price to pay.

DENIAL OF SELF-EXPRESSION.   There is a strong belief in organizations that we need to exercise self-control as well as to submit to the authority of those above us. When we are asked how we *feel* about something, the answer is "Who cares? We're here to get a job done; we're here to be rational and logical and to get on with the business at hand. This is no place to talk about feelings." In fact, one of the strongest terms of contempt is to say to somebody, "Let's not get into that touchy/feely stuff." How is it that touching and feeling have become such negative terms in organizational life? It is as if business is not personal. In fact, everything in business is personal, and should be. It is the major place where we spend our lives, and we all care deeply about what happens at work, both with the work to be done and the people around us. We pay a high price when we deny self-expression. All managers are constantly looking for ways to motivate and energize the people working for them. The source of all energy, passion, motivation, and an internally generated desire to do good work is our own *feeling* about what we are doing. To deny self-expression and ask people to exercise self-control and to behave themselves is to put a damper on their level of motivation and energy.

In the face of the dominant norms in most organizations that demand self-control, self-expression takes place in informal ways. People do talk about how they feel and about what's happening. Either after work, during lunch, or in the bathroom. The bathroom is the major place where self-expression is encouraged. If you really want to find out what's going on in the meeting, all you have to do is call a break and then hide in the bathroom and listen to people talk about the meeting. During the meeting itself, you ask, "How is it going?" and everybody says, "Just fine — this is a good meeting. I think it's important that we talk about history; I think it's important that we explore all the options and look at all the data that support the alternative positions we can take." You then call a break and go to the bathroom, and you hear people saying, "Can you believe what's going on in that meeting? I couldn't believe he said this, she said that. I think we should do something different — I feel what we're doing is a waste of time," and on and on and on.

Probably the most useful thing executives could do if they wanted to know how people were reacting to something in the organization would be to give up the comfortable privacy of their own bathroom, go and sit in a stall in one of the employee bathrooms, put their feet up so nobody knew they were in there, and sit and listen to people talk about what's going on in a meeting. The part of our employment contract that demands that we deny self-expression and exercise self-control restrains people's energy level and motivation and keeps us as managers from really understanding the impact of our actions on the internal motivation and energy of people to follow a path that we have laid out.

The fear we have, of course, is that if we encourage self-expression and deemphasize self-control, somehow the organization's purposes will be sacrificed, people will just do their own thing, and we will have an environment of self-indulgence and self-centeredness. This fear of losing control leads us to feel comfortable with a contract that denies self-expression, even if that wish for high control is at the expense of performance, motivation, energy, and what's good for building a business.

SACRIFICE FOR UNNAMED FUTURE REWARDS.   The third covenant of our contract is to make sacrifices. One manager put it very clearly: "Between Monday and Friday, I own them. The weekend is their own." When we ask people to sacrifice, we are, in essence, asking them to do something that if left to their own devices, they would choose not to do. We have the basic fear that what we ask people to do goes against the grain. When we demand sacrifice, we incur an obligation. In return for people's sacrifice, we imply the promise of a bright future. When they ask us to be more specific about what that future will look like, or what rewards will come their way, our response of necessity is "It's not something I can talk about right now." This belief in sacrifice is a basic element of our contract with employees and has led to a hidden bargain that we've all paid the price for. Many people joined large organizations out of a wish for safety and security and a long and comfortable future. There might have been a time when the organization could promise that kind of security and comfortable future, but that time has passed. Most large organizations are now getting smaller and smaller. Companies that for years never had a major layoff have had to let hundreds of people go.

When we fire people, in essence we violate this hidden bargain we have with our employees. We can no longer promise them that if they work hard, sacrifice, and commit themselves to our business, they'll always have a place here. The time of "bigger is better" and growth and expansion has passed. Even in the midst of a significant economic recovery, most organizations are getting smaller. To build a business based on people's sacrificing for the future gain is a very tenuous proposition.

BELIEF THAT THE ABOVE ARE JUST. It is not enough that we are expected to submit to authority, to deny self-expression, and to make sacrifices for unnamed future promises. We also have to believe that these three tenets of our contract are just and good for the organization. These three elements are dependency-creating forces. To believe that they are good for the business is to believe that dependency is good for the business. To express disbelief in the need to submit, sacrifice, and deny raises the specter of anarchy in those around us. The strongest wish of the organization is to maintain control at all costs, and this is the single most dominant value in pyramidal organizations.

The widespread belief in an external authority is that it's necessary to maintain order. If no strong lines of authority emanate from high places and outside the individual, then what we have is chaos. It's a law and order mind-set based on the belief that if people are left to their own instincts and their own authority, they'll somehow act in a way that runs counter to society and counter to the organization. We fear that people basically do not have the wish or the ability to act responsibly and that external authority must be constantly reinforced in order to keep us focused on common goals for the common purpose. This is essentially a pessimistic view of human nature. This pessimistic view says that essentially it is a jungle out there and we need to be very careful that things do not get out of hand. The assumption is that people are not able to exercise adequate self-control.

It is also a view that many of us have about ourselves. We

have come to believe that our own impulses and private personal issues may actually act as a disservice to the organization and therefore we need to be controlled externally. *We* need clear roles, responsibilities, and structure in order for *us* to be able to operate effectively.

There is evidence to support this belief; a good deal of conflict exists in organizations, and people around us at times do follow their own paths at the expense of the organization. If we choose to focus on others' self-centered behavior, this becomes a self-fulfilling prophecy. The more irresponsible behavior we see, the more tightly we control and the more firmly we believe that external authority is essential to achieve a purpose.

Our fear of anarchy is also expressed by one common complaint: lack of leadership. There is a chorus of statements that without strong, clear leadership, without people above pointing the direction and telling us how to operate, we cannot fulfill our goals or be the kind of employees that we want to be. It is almost a religious belief that control must come from the top and from outside ourselves for us to operate in a way that we are comfortable with.

High external control has the advantage of clarity and pays the price of allowing people not to take responsibility. That's the trade that's made. If we want clear structure, if we want clarity and simplicity of goals and purpose, and little disagreement about it, the easiest way to achieve that is through an autocratic high-control way of operating. People at the top always rationalize their controlling behavior by pointing to irresponsible acts at the bottom or middle of the organization.

In the extreme, it is the Franco rationale. Francisco Franco, as dictator of Spain, for years claimed that he would love to hold popular elections but that the people of Spain were just not ready for them. Managers, including ourselves, at every level use the same rationale. We say we would like to be more participative, we would like people to take more responsibility for themselves, we would like to create autonomous work teams, but people right now are not ready for this. What we see is our subordinate's wish for dependency, and we develop structures that respond to and reinforce that wish.

We also know that if we reduce the external control and give people more responsibility, the result will be some inefficiency. There is some truth in this. Some people, in fact, are not ready to take responsibility for their own actions or their own unit. Experiments have been conducted in organizations that give people more autonomy and more control. The immediate aftereffect of loosening control is a period of floundering, chaos, and lower productivity. People are so conditioned to operate in a highly structured environment that when some of the structure is taken away in the service of an entrepreneurial objective, there is a period in which people will test how much authority they have. They'll act in their own interest, and unpredictable events—some of which will not be in the best interests of the organization—will take place. It is easy then to conclude that the external control is needed. What we are ignoring is that unpredictable events not in the best interest of the organization also take place under highly controlled structures. The act of having a high-control, top-down organization in itself creates its own resistance. We're going to lose control in some sense no matter what kind of external structure we create.

In fact, the actual control the manager has over subordinates is somewhat of an illusion. A manager has every right to tell people what to do, but then, on their own, people decide whether they're going to do it.

Wartime events and sporting events are the common metaphors rationalizing the need for external authority. When pushed to the wall, the argument for high external control is always that if you're going to take the hill, you only want one platoon leader pointing the way. If you want to win a football game, you can only have room for one coach and for one person calling the plays. This Vince Lombardi mind-set dominates our culture and our organizations. We hold it tenaciously despite mounting evidence that high-control, autocratic, top-down systems are often less effective and less productive than more democratic participative systems. Even if an autocratic way of managing produces results, one of the unintended side effects of high external control is to increase people's feelings of dependency. If the wish is to create a more entrepreneurial organization, this core attitude about authority needs challenge and revision.

The alternative is to adopt the belief that the ultimate authority for our actions comes from within, that people are responsible for all of their actions despite what's happening in the culture and the environment around them. Despite the direction or lack of clarity of goals coming from above, despite the unpredictability of a marketplace, or the unique place in time and history that the organization finds itself in, ultimately, people make their own choices and the focus of control for their actions is internal.

The paradox is that our own efforts at maintaining control, maintaining authority, and denying self-expression fuel what instinct and fire does exist for other people to fight what we're trying to accomplish. In case after case of experiments in industry, when authority is reduced, when people are asked to do what makes sense to them rather than sacrifice, and when they're asked how they feel, performance goes up. Most of the successful experiments have been based on participative management and employee involvement. At the heart of these efforts has been a commitment by the managers to renegotiate the patriarchal contract. In many cases, performance has gone up and new plants have been started earlier than people thought possible. Failing units have revived and become satisfactory performers. Yet, often this happens in one pocket of the organization. The response of the rest of the organization is to look at the social experiment in a participative contract and say, "That may be fine for their situation, but it doesn't apply to us." The wish to maintain control is much stronger than the wish to increase performance. If managers have to choose between giving up control for the sake of higher performance and maintaining control knowing performance will be less, in most cases managers choose to maintain the control. This reinforces people's belief that their survival is dependent on the attitude and approval of their supervisor. It reinforces the belief that my own survival is something outside my own control, and not in my own hands, which is the essence of a dependent/bureaucratic mind-set. Organizations and managers are not solely to blame for the patriarchal contract because it takes two parties to make a contract. The patriarchal contract feeds the wish of each of us to be dependent, to be taken care of, and to submit to a higher authority. To not have to be responsible for our lives or our actions. It's a willing union between those of us with authority who hold onto it tightly and those who work for us who want somehow to avoid the responsibility of creating an organization themselves.

MYOPIC SELF-INTEREST: THE MYTH THAT ADVANCEMENT AND SELF-ESTEEM ARE RELATED

The second element in the bureaucratic cycle is myopic self-interest. In its simplest sense, politics is the pursuit of self-interest. I seek power and influence for a purpose. How I define self-interest is critical. The traditional definition of self-interest is that what I want from work is to get ahead. If you ask me why I work, I say, "To pay the mortgage." The easier it is for me to pay the mortgage, the better I am doing. We have also bought the belief that self-esteem and advancement are related. The higher I go in the organization, the better I will feel about myself. My career success is expressed by my altitude in the hierarchy. This basic belief—that advancement and winning the approval of those above is what really motivates people and gives meaning to their work—is deeply ingrained in all of us. There is a need to question this belief and take the rather radical position that this very definition of success is part of the problem. When self-interest gets defined as

- being promoted into the winner's circle,

- winning the approval of those above us,

- receiving significant salary increases,

- creating safety and security in our place in the organization,

- having more and more people and functions under our control,

then we set into motion forces that inevitably create a bureau-cratic mentality and manipulative way of operating. If we are serious about creating entrepreneurs and positive politics, we have to challenge these beliefs about self-interest. From child-hood we have been presented with images and messages that the acquisition of material things is a goal worth striving for. "The man who dies with the most toys wins." As managers we often rely on our subordinates' wish to get ahead as a means of controlling them. The essence of performance evaluation is using the threat or promise of influencing people's salary, promotion, and safety in order to get subordinates to operate in ways that we desire. We use these personal, tangible rewards as ways of making sure the organization goals get met. And it works.

The problem is that we pay a price for this tremendous emphasis on personal payoff as a motivational device. Funda-mentally, it creates a dependency that often does not serve the business. What follows are some ways in which self-centered definition of self-interest interferes with what we are trying to create in the organization.

MYOPIC SELF-INTEREST NO. 1: ADVANCEMENT. If advancement is one of our goals, let's look, in an admittedly overstated way, at what life at the top offers us. There is almost universal acceptance of the belief that it is a good thing to get ahead in the organization. It's worth examining both the goal itself and the trip to get there.

We want to be promoted, to have more responsibility, to have control over more people; in other words, the more power we have, the better off we are. In the United States we have no kings or queens, no royalty. In the place of royalty, the aristocracy of our culture are the chief executives of our major corporations. These CEOs are the heroes of corporate existence. The ultimate dream of advancement is realized when you never have to drive your own car, carry no personal cash or even credit cards, and are relieved from having to fly on commercial airlines. This life of power and privilege is romanticized on the pages of *Forbes* and *Fortune* magazines. If you work in a large city, your limousine picks you up at 6:00 A.M. and whisks you silently to work behind smoke-colored windows, with a telephone at your side and a reading lamp over your shoulder.

You arrive at work at a private garage entrance of a tall glass and steel building. A quick greeting to the security guard, calling him by his first name, and up you go in a key-driven private elevator to the top floor for another hard day at the office.

The executive floor is our goal. It gives the illusion of quiet and peace. The decor is understated elegance, the lighting indirect, punctuated by beautiful Williamsburg table lamps, mahogany desks, and expensive modern art, all floating on a sea of beige or light blue carpeting.

The executive secretaries serve as the palace guard, no less erect or imperturbable than their counterparts at Buckingham Palace. The major function of the executive secretary is to demonstrate loyalty to the executive by controlling access.

The crowning symbol of life at the top is the typical boardroom. Most boardrooms are designed as the ultimate expression of power. They are filled with long, narrow, unmovable tables. The atmosphere is very formal and serious. Those making presentations to the board are treated like subjects appearing at court.

While the boardroom is Mount Everest, other forms of

corporate jewelry lure us in our climb up the ladder. We pay great attention to how we furnish our office. The way you know how you're doing in an organization is best symbolized by your desk. The question here is how large is your overhang. The overhang is the opposite side of your desk, where other people sit when they're meeting with you. The more of another person's body that you can fit underneath the opposite side of your desk, the larger the overhang and the better you're doing in the organization. If you rise high enough in the organization, you get a dining room table as a desk. This means that the desk is all overhang, that there are no drawers, no clutter, no mess. Simply a large dining room table to symbolize the extent to which the organization values what you're doing.

Another sign of success is a private bathroom. I remember meeting with an executive once and being told by the secretary that he was waiting for me. I walked into the office and found no one there. After standing around for a while, wondering if I was losing it and looking behind the desk thinking that perhaps something had happened or the executive was hiding from me, all of a sudden the wall opened and the executive walked out of a hidden door in the wall. I said, "Where have you been?" And he said, "Going to the bathroom." He then showed me the private bathroom and shower that had been provided for him.

Great attention is also paid to office size and corner windows. Each office is carefully controlled by size and number of modules according to level. The more modules you have, the bigger the office and, of course, the better off you are. The more your office looks like a living room, the better you're doing in the organization. To meet with the top executive is to sit on a couch or around a coffee table with beautiful paintings and personal effects surrounding you, talking about business. What always bothered me was the fact that these executive offices were furnished more nicely than my own home.

So what is the problem with this life-style and environment of those who have made it to the top? From a distance they look great. Up close it is another story. In many ways, this is a life of isolation, extreme self-sacrifice, and vulnerability. Yesterday an executive near the top of a large corporation commented that it was possible for him to come to work, go up in the elevator, work in his office all day, eat lunch in the private dining room, and go home without ever talking to another human being except his secretary. He has to make a special note to himself to get out of the office and the executive tower once a week just to stay a little bit in touch with the rest of the organization.

The top executive, surrounded with comfort and privilege justly earned, pays a price in the isolation and distance it creates from those below. Executive privilege and decor act as a visual reminder of the status and power difference between the executive and those who come up to meet to do business. What is a tangible reward to the executive serves as a reminder to the subordinate of the dependency relationship that exists. In the face of this, the executive has a hard time finding out what is really going on in the organization. We are all reluctant at best to communicate bad news to those who hold our future in their hands. The symbols of power vividly reinforce this.

The boardroom, the ultimate meeting place of those who have reached the pinnacle, is about as relaxed as the intensive care unit at a hospital. The top managers of an organization want to know what is happening down below, want people to communicate honestly with them, and want to make decisions based on real information, and yet when they are together as a group, they operate in an environment that makes genuine human interaction extremely difficult.

To be at the top is also to live in a fishbowl. Every act, every statement (in one situation I was in, every sigh) is watched carefully for clues and messages about where we or our projects stand. The expectations people have of their leaders in a bureaucratic system are unreal and constraining. In a paradoxical way, having too much power makes top executives more controlled by the people under them than the other way around.

Job security at the top is also overrated. In one large health care company made up of fifty or so smaller companies, the average tenure of a company president is slightly over two years. This in itself is somewhat disconcerting, but the problem at the top is that the organization has no place to put past presidents. The consequence of falling out of favor is much more severe for those at the top than for those at lower levels. Workers can be transferred, hidden, or trained. If you are at the top and stumble, it's career reevaluation time. Even if you fall with a golden parachute, you are still going to hit the ground, and it hurts every time.

The bottom line is that life at the top looks good at a distance, but seen and experienced up close, it serves to create the bureaucratic and political mentality that top executives constantly complain about. The pressures, isolation, and competitiveness at the top drive people to worry much more about maintaining what they have, act with undue caution, and feel much more dependent than their position would seem to warrant. The paradox is that it is rare when you find a willingness to risk and a choice for autonomy at the top of the organization. Anyone who has a job that allows him or her to work at all levels of the organization realizes that the higher in the pyramid one goes, the greater the caution, secretiveness, and politicking. At times it seems that at the top of many organizations increased negative politics and running for office are the norm. The more we have in tangible rewards, the more we want to hold onto them. As we move up the organization, we become more concerned about what we have to lose than what we are trying to create.

The alternative is roughly to equalize privileges and symbols of status up and down the organization. Make everybody's office the same size, with the same furniture, the same kind of pictures on the wall, the same number of windows. The message this gives is that the intention here is not to build an empire or to create a comfortable life-style for oneself. The intention is to build an organization.

The success of the organization should be the primary basis

for rewarding people, not individual enhancements. We too often put tremendous emphasis on individual compensation and trappings and then complain that people are only self-serving and out to advance themselves. It is self-defeating for organizations to do too many things to reward people for being self-centered and defining their self-interest in terms of moving up in the organization We do this because we think we need to in order to control people and to keep them engaged in our business. We bought the myth that getting ahead is what it's all about. It's not.

If people at the bottom or middle of the organization assume that things will get better for them only as they move up the ladder, it is an assumption worth reexamining. The belief that self-esteem and advancement are positively related is in many ways a myth. There is no assurance that if we please our boss and get promoted, we will feel better about ourself or feel more in control of our life. This becomes clearer as we look at other forms of self-interest.

MYOPIC SELF-INTEREST NO. 2: SEEKING APPROVAL.   If our ultimate goal is to reach the top and enjoy the elegant life-style that offers, we are then destined to spend our career seeking the approval of those above us. On the surface this seems normal and natural. Our entire experience with institutions has taught us that to be successful, we have to please people in power. Moving through the school system was the most vivid example. The measure of performance in school was our grades. Students get good grades by pleasing their teachers. At times it seems like getting good grades becomes more important than learning. Students size up the teacher early in the semester and decide what they are going to have to do for this teacher to get the grade they want. This is called being maze bright. In the extreme, students avoid those courses in which they have an interest but the grapevine tells them are very difficult. In the early 1900s, grades were developed to evaluate how well the teacher was teaching. Somehow that got turned around so that grades now measure the student, and the grade-point average has become the goal in and of itself. Grades become a measure of a teacher's approval, and students engage in all kinds of elaborate choreography to get that approval. This became clear to me when I would ask my own children how a class was going. Regardless of their age or subject matter, their answer was always the same—either "The teacher likes me" or "The teacher does not like me." When I pressed for some reaction to course content, it seemed a matter of indifference. The teacher likes me. The teacher does not like me. End of discussion. After twelve to sixteen years of this acculturation, employees enter the organization ready to move through another approval-seeking system. The organization doesn't disappoint them. You might ask, "What is so wrong with seeking the approval and support of those around us, including our boss?" The problem arises to the extent that others' approval becomes the driving force in our actions. If we are constantly focused on seeking others' approval, almost to the exclusion of what we personally think is best for the business, then we run the risk of sacrificing the integrity of our own function for the sake of finding the most popular path. We are not in business to gain others' approval; we are here to get work done, work that moves the business forward—even if at times our forward progress is upsetting to those around us. Approval as a dominant value is an expression of our dependency and gives rise to the feeling that our survival is in someone else's hands. This overriding concern for approval manifests itself in several different ways.

We are reluctant to communicate bad news up the line for fear the messenger will be shot. One large research and development company commissioned a study of major projects that had failed. The findings revealed that very early in the life of these projects, key scientists knew that the promise of the projects would never be fulfilled. The scientists were asked why they didn't raise the red flag early in the game. The answer was that they felt that so much money had been budgeted and such strong promises had been made, that if they cried out that the emperor had no clothes, they would be limiting their careers. Better to maintain the approval of those above than to try to stop a locomotive well under way.

Dialogue with top management becomes an extremely well rehearsed event. To talk to someone two or three levels above us means we have to have all our ducks in order. We have to be buttoned up and battened down. We have to make sure that we can answer every question we are asked. We have JIC (just in case) files to make sure that we look like we are on top of things. In some organizations people can't have a meeting unless their ideas are outlined on overhead transparencies. Some of this is useful and does facilitate communication. In many cases though, it is overdone and tends to create such structure and formality in a dialogue that real communication, especially about sensitive issues, hardly has a chance. When our need to look good overrides our need for honest communication, then our deeper purpose of building an organization of our own choosing has been deflected.

In our desire for approval, we sometimes make promises that we probably can't fulfill. We agree to a schedule or to a level of quality out of a need to avoid a painful confrontation. We live with the feeling that we cannot say no to others' demands, particularly if the demands come from a higher level than our own. The inability to say no results in our making unrealistic commitments, and this in turn requires our own unit to twist itself inside out. Other people base their plans on our commitments, and when we cannot fulfill our promise, despite our superhuman effort, every other group down the line is thrown off balance.

As managers we look at the approval-seeking behavior beneath us and have very ambivalent feelings about it. On the one hand, it is reassuring and right that people affirm our position of authority and come looking for our approval. If they didn't, we would fear some sort of anarchy, with everyone going off in a different direction. Our subordinates' need for approval becomes the instrument for maintaining control over our unit. As managers we also need support from our own unit, and we perceive our subordinates' wish to please us as evidence of their commitment to the objectives that we have established.

The other side of the coin is that we want our people to take responsibility for making our department successful. We want them to be independent and to make their own decisions. We express this wish by asking them to come to us with solutions, not problems. Independence and approval-seeking behavior do not fit together very well. The struggle for us as managers is that if we really want to build a strong, self-sufficient organization under us, we need to encourage our people to confront and push against us. In the long run, having people believe that approval-seeking actions are in their personal self-interest works against the kind of self-starting internal commitment that is needed to build the business.

MYOPIC SELF-INTEREST NO. 3: HARD CASH.   The universal measure of our worth to the organization is how much we are paid. This is true at every level. The same attention is given to how much the chief executive officer is paid as is given to the wage of the hourly worker. It is a source of corporate pride that the president makes $1.5 million a year. The press widely reports the details of the golden parachutes America's corporate aristocracy receive when they change jobs. To hire top executives, organizations not only have to pay them a million dollars a year but have to give them an employment contract that guarantees their employment for a five-year period. They become as wealthy if they are fired as they would had they successfully stayed on the job. What is meaningful about this is the simple fact that monetary compensation is universally used as the measure of value of the person.

At other levels of the organization tremendous emphasis is given to how much each person's salary increase is every year. People argue and complain bitterly for hours if they get a 7.2 percent increase instead of a 7.6 percent increase. The belief is that four-tenths of a percent of pay is not only important in itself but that it is also a measure of equity, fairness, how much the organization values what we do. It has more symbolic meaning than it has substance. The actual differential increase between the average performer and the high performer generally is quite small, maybe $1,000 to $2,000 a year. All that really means, given the high progressive tax rate we have, is that we start working for the government earlier in the afternoon. For example, since a fairly heavy proportion of the increase is eaten up by federal income taxes, for me to get a large increase means I start working for the government at 2:20 in the afternoon instead of 2:40 in the afternoon. All the work I do after 2:40 in the afternoon goes to pay taxes. (This may be why people do their best work in the morning—because they're working for themselves.)

Another measure of the importance given to pay is all the effort that is expended by personnel departments on salary surveys and trying to maintain equity in the pay system. In fact, a major purpose of compensation systems is to maintain equity across the organization. Elaborate measures are taken to make sure people are paid roughly the same amount across different divisions of a company. Outside of the sales function, pay is rarely related to performance. In a way that's OK because there is little evidence that performance goes up when pay goes up.

Another aspect of compensation systems is the fact that the decision about how much an individual's pay will be raised is made between twelve and eighteen months before the person actually receives the pay increase. Sometime in the fall, a salary budget is determined, people are rated on their level of performance, and an increase corresponding to that performance is determined for the following year. This means deciding in October whether a person is going to get paid an increase sometime next summer or fall. This lag time between the decision about a pay increase and the actual receiving of the increase almost ensures the fact that what a person gets paid is only marginally related to how well that person is performing.

There are times when an individual is performing very well in the summer of the year and yet receives a small increase because the year before the person's performance was questionable. At other times the individual is slacking off, indifferent, and slow to respond to requests and yet receives a pay increase designed for a high performer some months before.

The beautiful thing about salary as a measure of value is that it is so tangible. It's a number that we hold onto, we can talk about, we can compare across divisions and across companies and never mind whether it's real or an illusion or symbolic. It's people's most common topic of conversation and the most tangible measure of how they're doing in the organization. The mere fact that people are so focused on their pay as a measure is an expression in and of itself of the bureaucratic mind that pervades most of our organizational life.

Salary is also a beautiful rationalization to hide other difficulties we have as managers. Every time any of our valued people leave our organization and work for someone else, we are guaranteed the comfort of explaining their leaving by the fact that they got more money in their new job. I've rarely heard a supervisor or manager say that a subordinate quit the company because the subordinate was not happy in the job, didn't like the way the organization was managed, found no meaning in the work, or felt the supervision was inadequate. The universal excuse is that the subordinate left for more pay. This is the manager's way of saying to the world if my valued people leave, it's not my fault.

This explanation is given credence by the fact that people almost always get a salary increase if they change jobs. The marketplace always values our skills more highly than our own organization does. As managers we are always willing to pay more money for somebody we don't know than for somebody whom we know and whose limitations and weaknesses are visible to us.

The point here is that the emphasis on pay is a symptom of the bureaucratic mind-set. The fact that we care so much about how we are paid is a measure of our discouragement about the quality, meaning, and integrity of work and the contribution that we're able to make on the job. If we thought we were doing work that had meaning, substance, and depth, the issue of pay would be a quiet one. In some ways, the emphasis we put on pay is a measure of our despair. We say that if we can't do meaningful work and we can't be a part of an organization that we truly believe in, then we want to be paid a lot for the sacrifice we are making.

Since pay has become a measure of how much approval we receive from the organization, the emphasis on salary encourages our self-interest's being defined in dependent, approval-seeking ways. When self-interest is defined in terms of the kind of work we're doing and the kind of contribution we're making, pay is much less of an issue. If you look at organizations that have a purpose and goal of service and contribution, such as health care and voluntary agencies, the pay is always very low, and yet many talented people stay in those jobs.

The effect of tangible rewards and corporate jewelry is the exact opposite of the intention. The intention is to help us feel valued and rewarded for what we are doing. The intention is to help us feel better about ourselves and the contribution we are making.

The price we pay for elaborate compensation systems, beautiful working conditions, and daytime comforts is that we begin to believe that we need these things. We begin to value ourselves according to how many of the company's rewards are being handed out to us. This simply reinforces our feeling of dependency, increases our feeling of being trapped by a pair of golden handcuffs, and deflects our attention away from doing work that has meaning and creating an organization of our own choosing.

MYOPIC SELF-INTEREST NO. 4: THE WISH TO BE SAFE.   In addition to advancement, approval, and pay, the fourth characteristic of a pyramidal organization is the pervasive desire for safety. Our daily actions are driven by the wish to remain safe and free from blame. As long as it's not our fault, who cares what happens. Meetings take up so much of our time because they are devoted to defending our position and establishing our innocence. There is a saying that in therapy all of the most important statements are made in the first ten minutes and the last ten minutes. In the first ten minutes we express what we are worried about, and in the last ten minutes, faced with the imminent ending of our session, we begin to tell the truth. If the therapy session lasts fifty minutes, we use the middle thirty minutes to blame others, talk about how tough our life is, and explain how we have done everything humanly possible and it still hasn't worked.

The same with meetings at work. We begin by setting the agenda and then proceed to explain the history, background, studies, data, options and their consequences, and the roles everyone has played in the melodrama. All of this discussion is designed to give us a feeling of security that we are doing the right things and that we are proceeding in a reasonable and rational way that no one could find fault with. This is our wish to be safe. Luckily, meetings do have an ending time, so in the last few minutes, we decide what to do. Maybe. When we do decide, our decision is based on hunch, intuition, subjective feeling, or the dominance of one or two personalities.

Unfortunately for us at work, instead of fifty minutes, meetings last for hours. Much of the wasted energy at work is a response to the desire to be safe and blame-free. Task forces, additional studies, outside consultants, committees often are merely expressions of our caution. Caution and safety are the antithesis of being entrepreneurial and political in a positive way. As with advancement and control, the wish for safety is largely frustrated and beyond our grasp. There is really no safe way.

At one point, if we joined a large organization, we knew we were giving up some of our autonomy, but we thought we were buying security in exchange. I'll go to work for the government, AT&T, or a Fortune 500 company because these organizations offer stable, long-term employment. This is no longer true. AT&T's divestiture symbolizes the reality that there is no longer any place to hide. We read in the paper that Ma Bell—our own mother, no less—is outplacing 24,000 people. If you are not safe working for AT&T, where are you safe?

The change in the Coca-Cola formula was another traumatic assault on our cocoon. If Coke is forced to change its formula after ninety-nine years, is anything sacred? The company received over 500,000 phone calls complaining about the change. Coke employees were subjected to verbal abuse wherever they went — even in church — for the formula change. Was this uproar really over taste? Not at all. It was in part a cry of outrage against loss of tradition, against unpredictability and the fact that there is little outside ourselves to hold onto.

The desire to be safe and free from blame comes out in little ways, such as when you ask people how they're doing and they reply, "Not bad." "Not bad" means no one is on our case. Again, the wish to be blame-free, safe, is bureaucratic in nature. It is behind our efforts to be clever, strategic, and manipulative in our dealings with others. It underlies the wish to pursue our self-interest in ways that ruffle no one's feathers. It creates a language of "touching base, trial balloons, running it up the flagpole."

Being political in a positive way is to accept danger and move toward the edge. No easy task, but the safety we are giving up isn't really there.

MYOPIC SELF-INTEREST NO. 5: CONTROL AT ALL COSTS.

Now hear this
Now hear this
This is the captain speaking
This is the captain speaking
That is all
That is all
    Old navy proverb

To live in an organizational pyramid is to pay great attention to control. At times it seems we value control above all else.

Whole departments and whole levels of management are created simply for the purpose of keeping control. It is as though if we lose control, we've lost everything. As long as we are in control, who cares what else is happening.

Most current experiments in productivity improvement focus on giving employees more control over their work. The press is full of success stories about worker involvement, quality circles, autonomous work groups, flat organizations, all operating under the heading of participative management. Despite the positive publicity and real results of these approaches, they are by far the exception. Even when a major automobile manufacturer like Ford Motor Company commits itself to employee involvement right from the top, the transformation from autocratic to participative management takes years and years.

Why is this? Because we have learned to value control above all else. If you give someone the choice between low control/high performance on the one hand and high control/low performance on the other hand, the common response is "Thank you for the interesting information, but I will continue to take the high-control/low-performance alternative."

Another expression of our passion for control is our disdain for surprise. "You can do what makes sense to you, be master of your own fate, but whatever you do, don't surprise me." You can tell many managers that over the weekend the roof collapsed, the employees welded the doors shut, and the receptionist ran off with the security guard, and their response will be, "That doesn't surprise me." As long as we are not surprised, we create the illusion that we are in control. The desire for control through lack of surprises is in many ways a loss—to the person and to the organization. The case for surprise is quite straightforward:

- In research, surprise is essential to high performance. The essence of discovery is to be surprised. To not be surprised is to miss discoveries and inventions.

- All learning is preceded by a moment of ignorance, followed by a moment of surprise. When we avoid surprises, we avoid risks, which prevents us from finding new ways of doing business.

- Surprise also gives seasoning to the quality of our experience. Excitement, adventure, and the unknown are sources of motivation and energy. No surprises is a way of bleeding energy and motivation from our work lives.

Despite these rational arguments for surprise, which are arguments for loosening control, the machinery is deeply institutionalized for creating organizations of absolute predictability and control. Setting goals and measurable objectives and working according to plan are the lifeblood of most organizational cultures. The paradox is that while we value planning and prediction with religious zeal, we know in our hearts that they are not possible. The most common complaint for inadequate performance is lack of planning, lack of clear goals, lack of adequate controls. This yearning for control is a central theme of life in a pyramid and is also what helps create the bureaucratic style and negative political activities that we wish to change. If we wish to move our organizations in an entrepreneurial direction, we have no choice but to seriously confront our values and attitudes about maintaining control.

What we have working in our favor is that the wish for control is mostly an illusion anyway. If we think we have control over fifty or a thousand or twenty thousand people, we are kidding ourselves. The inmates do run the prison. The people at the bottom are the ones who decide every day what work gets done. If those at the bottom want to fight the organization, all they have to do is to enforce the rules and regulations. This is the bureaucratic form of revenge. If the police want to go on strike but are forbidden by law to do so, all they have to do to shut down the city is to enforce the law. The technical term for this is *corporate gridlock*. The people who work for us decide what gets done. We don't. We tell them what we want to get done, but they decide whether and how to do it. And the cruel trick is that the higher in the organization we go, the less contact we have with the touchable work of the organization.

The higher we are, the more dependent we are upon layers on layers of the organization to find out what is really going on. Top executives get so frustrated trying to discover the truth about what is happening beneath them that they bring in staff groups to act as their agents. This is why so many corporate staff groups grow so large. Top managers, frustrated with their lack of information and control, create staff auditors, planners, trainers to circumvent the normal channels. These groups are a wish on the part of executives to maintain control but also an acknowledgment that they don't have the control.

Those at the top do have the power to give direction and focus, to hire and fire, to make decisions about dollars, people, technology. But the actual control to make those decisions work is, in reality, out of their grasp.

In order to create an entrepreneurial culture, where people are political in the best sense, we must give up some of our control. We can take comfort in the fact that we are only giving up something that we never really had in the first place. We can't lose something that we don't have. Deemphasizing control and keeping it in its proper perspective is not giving up something real; it is only giving up the illusion, which isn't such a bad thing.

MANIPULATIVE TACTICS

We can now focus on traditional political behavior. As stated earlier, politics as we know it can be characterized by

- maneuvering situations and, at times, people,

- managing information and plans carefully to our own advantage,

- being strategic and instrumental in our relationships,

- seeking approval of those above us,

- being cautious in telling the truth.

These kinds of activities, which are the essence of bureaucratic behavior, are driven and if not created then supported by the nature of our contract with the organization plus the way we define our self-interest.

Given a patriarchal contract that places primary emphasis on control and a definition of self-interest that gives primary attention to safety and winning the approval of those above us, the unavoidable consequence is that we manage through manipulation. This is the third element of the bureaucractic cycle. Manipulation is so ingrained in the way we operate that we often don't even know we are engaging in it. Manipulation is the act of trying to control other people without their knowing it. There is a difference between control and manipulation. Control occurs when we guide other people's behavior and let them know that we are doing so. Manipulation occurs when we try to influence others and act as if we are not.

Manipulation is an emotion-laden word. Most of us would reject the more blatant forms of using other people to our own advantage. Machiavelli, the master manipulator, would probably have difficulty finding a job in most modern organizations. Bureaucratic political acts are not so clear as outright lying, using others and then discarding them, destroying our enemies or befriending falsely those we have contempt for.

The politics we are most likely to be part of are more subtle and have evolved as coping strategies rather than acts of aggression. We reluctantly become manipulative because we are bouncing back and forth between (1) knowing what is needed to get our job done and becoming advocates for our own unit and (2) living in a high-control, approval-seeking culture in which people's own upward mobility is constantly at the center of their consciousness. Being indirect, clever, and closed is an adaptive response to our predicament and not really our first choice in how we would like to operate. We become manipulative at first because it works and seems so well accepted. After a while, we become part of and carriers of a culture that initially we viewed with puzzlement.

What follows are some of the more subtle ways in which negative politics is enacted. Seeing these clearly makes it easier for us to choose an alternative, more positive path.

SAYING WHAT WE DON'T MEAN. Essentially, manipulation is saying yes when we mean no. People come to us with ideas and proposals and our response is "It's a very interesting idea." *Interesting* is the word we most commonly use to express either our indifference or our objection while acting as if we want to be supportive. It's what your mother-in-law says about where you place the sofa in your living room when she can't stand the choice you've made. She walks in and says, "It's very interesting where you have placed the sofa and how you have re-arranged the room." This is her code for saying the place looks awful!

When we make proposals to people and their response is "We need to study it more," or "We need to refer it to a task force," or "We need to set up a committee," or "We need to check with other people to see how they feel about it," they are, in essence, saying that our idea is not one that they can support, but they can't tell us that they can't support it. The response "The timing isn't right; I think this would better be done in the third quarter of next year" is organizational code for saying no but acting like the answer might at some future time be yes. All of these are subtle forms of manipulation.

GOD IS MY ALLY. Another form of manipulation is name-dropping. People come to you trying to persuade you to do something, and in the course of the conversation, they happen to mention that one of the top executives supports the idea. If the top executive's name is Jack, they will, as an aside, mention that they were talking with Jack about this the other day and Jack thought it was a good idea. In fact when they tell you that they and Jack were together last week, one evening, on vacation, at the summer home that they own jointly, celebrating the anniversary of the marriage of their children—and Jack happened to mention that this was a good idea—they are letting you know that you're facing into gale-force pressure. To communicate the implied or expressed support of people not in the room is an indirect way of trying to control other people's actions. It's common, and it works.

UNDERSTATING THE DOWNSIDE.   A third form of manipulation is to express one side of the story or to shade our own doubts. We make proposals expressing the benefits to the organization and all the reasons that it will work, and we understate the risk and the doubts that we have about it. Too often we act as if we have no doubts and try to control the outcome by withholding the fact that there's a risk to any action taken. To not express the reasons against our own proposal is a way to maneuver the other person into supporting us.

COMMUNICATION DEVICES.   A more subtle form of manipulation is the use of interpersonal techniques to try to get our way. All of us have been to workshops on listening skills and how to manage interviews. We've all learned to make eye contact, lean forward with our elbow on our knee, and show interest. We've learned to restate other people's positions in ways that are acceptable to them. These techniques are useful if they're actually used for listening or maintaining contact. Often, though, they're misused as influence strategies. When I use an indirect influence strategy on you as a way of helping you feel understood and to win your support, I'm just engaging in a more sophisticated form of manipulation.

PADDING.   Another common form of manipulation is padding our demands, knowing that we'll get less than we ask for. This is what budgeting is all about. We are constantly trying to present the case and project future figures in a way that expresses optimism and in a way that if ever we get less than what we ask for, we'll get closer to what we think we really need.

LANGUAGE THAT MASKS REALITY.   The most powerful form of manipulation is the attempt to use language that masks reality. Meetings are constantly being held to try to figure out how to communicate bad news in a way that people will find acceptable. The executives of a large bank decided to cut the corporate staff by 40 percent. Their feeling was if they told people their intentions, it would be demoralizing to the organization. So, instead, they called the process the Delta Project, and it was positioned as a project to "engage people in the process of reexamining their function and their mission and their real purpose for existing." Those involved knew that the intent was to cut back on home office staff because the executives introduced the project by stating explicitly that their intent was not just to cut back on home office staff.

All of the phrases we use to introduce statements that deny what's to follow are subtle forms of manipulation. We say, "I don't mean to interrupt you"; we say, "I don't want you to be upset about what I'm trying to say"; we say, "I don't mean to rationalize my actions; I don't mean to be defensive or to justify what I'm about to do."

All of these statements are designed to talk others out of their natural response to our actions and, in effect, tip off the real intent. As managers, we spend a tremendous amount of time positioning the messages we send to our employees. Many companies have communication departments whose whole purpose is to position the messages from top management. Any effort at positioning is really a desire to make people feel better about what we are about to communicate than they naturally would. It's an effort to seduce people out of their discouragement or resentment.

It is fun sometimes just to listen for the code that people talk in when they don't want the other person to know their true position. In cynical moments, I call them organizational lies; in moments of generosity, I see them as expressions of the caution we feel about being direct with one another.

"Thank you for the feedback." When people give us bad news or express their disappointment in our actions, we feel obligated to act interested and even grateful. We say, "Thank you for the feedback." This is code for the fact that we hate what they just told us, it is upsetting to us, we disagree with them totally, but instead of getting into a long harangue, we will terminate the discussion quickly by expressing appreciation and giving the impression that we are interested in learning about our own mistakes — from them.

"I am just here to be helpful." This is most often used by people from the corporate staff when they are visiting a division. The relationship between the corporate staff and the field staff is tenuous at best and everyone knows this. Field people think corporate people exist only to evaluate, judge, and report back to top management areas that need improvement. People from the corporate staff think that people in the field want total independence and the right to run their own division or office any way they please. Corporate people are also convinced that field people are narrow in their interests and do not have the good of the total organization at heart. With this natural tension in mind, the corporate person — thinking, "I know you don't want me to be here, and in fact I'm not too thrilled about being here either" — says, "I'm here to be helpful!"

"We are glad to have you here." This is said by people in the field or an operating unit to those from corporate/home offices. It is also said to consultants for the same reasons. The bedrock of field people's self-esteem is their ability to solve problems on their own. They don't really want any help from outsiders. But field people aren't stupid; they know they have to endure a certain amount of outside interference. They figure they can minimize the damage done by the corporate people by feigning enthusiasm. Thus the statement "We are glad to have you here." The more sophisticated field people follow up this opening statement by asking, "How was your trip down, where are you staying, where did you have dinner last night,"

and most important, "when are you heading back?" This is the field person's code for thinking, "There is no real reason for your being here, but if I can distract you by my hospitality, it will dilute the purported reason for your visit."

"People are our most important asset." Every organization claims that people are number one. If that is true, why in hard times are people the first to go? Even in the midst of economic recoveries, many organizations contract their work forces as severely as they can. The reason is that for most organizations, labor is their major controllable cost. Despite the pain in doing so, we lay off people for economic reasons. People, in fact, are not number one. Economics is. People are probably number six. Economics is numbers one, two, and three; capital equipment is number four; technology is number five. Then comes the working class. The problem is not that people are number six. The problem is that we say that people are number one mostly for effect. We may have the wish that people come first, but to say it creates an expectation that we cannot fulfill. To keep proclaiming that people are number one when, for good reason, it is not true, is another form of deception.

"I am offering you a developmental opportunity." When your boss offers you a "developmental opportunity," beware. It is a way of telling you that he or she is not happy with what you are doing and wants to move you somewhere else. Calling the move a developmental opportunity is a way to keep you from being upset about the change. Of course, some changes are good for our development; it is the subtle positioning of the reason for the change that is manipulative.

"I have confidence in you." When others tell you that they really have confidence in you, ask yourself why they are so concerned and doubtful about you. We only choose to communicate confidence in those people that we are concerned about. If we are truly confident about something, the thought of talking about our confidence never occurs to us. We only communicate confidence out of the instinct to shore up something that is faltering. Our unquestioned belief that we have to control, shape, motivate, guide those around us (especially our sub-

ordinates) is an indication of how much manipulative acts have invaded the fabric of our relationships. It becomes a subtle way of treating others as if they were children, unable to handle the reality of events. The bind is that we cannot treat our subordinates like children and at the same time expect them to take responsibility for the success and future of our unit.

"You are the accidental victim of a downsizing process." No one gets fired anymore. Because of discomfort with playing God and employees' legal rights, we go to great lengths to find other words for getting rid of people we don't want.

Being fired is a form of dying, and it becomes hard to know who has shot us or how. I have been collecting words that are used to keep people from thinking they have been fired, even though they are out of work. The beauty of these words is that they have a neutral, institutional, almost noble quality to them.

- You are the accidental victim of a *downsizing* process.

- There is a *dislodgement* taking place, of which you are a part.

- We have *rebundled* the organization.

- Our *deselection* committee has nominated you.

- That person has been *booked* (banker's term for writing off a bad loan).

- Welcome to the *Golden Years Program* (code for forced early retirement).

- You have been *dehired* and *decruited*.

My favorite is a major New York bank's Career Progression Review (CPR); it means you are going to be fired. If you are smart, when they call you up to schedule your CPR, tell them you will be out of town for six months.

All of these terms blur the reality of what is happening. Because certain employees have only been deselected, downsized, rebundled, dislodged, we don't feel so bad and neither should they. We are eliminating jobs, not people. Because these terms disguise reality, they are manipulative. The manipulation is designed to finesse fired employees out of normal resentment and negative feelings they might have about the organization. We want them to leave, but we don't want them to be angry with us.

How people get fired is also carefully thought through. In the more primitive organizations, employees are exiled as soon as they are told. They are asked to be out of the building by the end of the day. Sometimes a security guard is waiting for them at their office to watch them pack and to make sure they take only what is theirs. One of the large broadcasting networks in New York fired a vice president by having someone meet him at the elevator in the morning and telling him it was no longer necessary for him to go to his office. Once people are no longer on the payroll and under a firm's control, they are seen as potentially bad apples, poised and eager to spoil and corrupt those around them. Most firings are done on Friday afternoon, giving people the weekend to cool down and get reasonable before contacting other employees.

Most organizations, however, are more sophisticated in their firing practices. Nowadays after employees get the bad news, they walk out of the boss's office and there waiting for them is the corporate funeral director—their personal outplacement counselor. Dressed in dark suits, with a look of compassion in their eyes, these counselors are there to help fired people work through the five stages of dying. They tell these people that right now they are experiencing denial; they can't believe it is happening to them. The next stage is bargaining. "I will do anything to get my job back. Why didn't they give me more warning? If they would give me another chance, things would be different." Then comes, "Why me? There are hundreds of other employees who don't do half the job that I do." The fourth stage is anger. "How could they do this to me? I'll show them. Where is my lawyer?" The fifth and final stage is acceptance. "There is nothing I can do about being laid off, and in fact, tomorrow is the first day of the rest of my life. This experience gives me the opportunity, in the midstream of my existence, to redecide how I want to spend the rest of my work life." The goal of the outplacement counselor is to get the former employee through the anger to acceptance as soon as possible. It is good for the employee, and it minimizes the number of lawsuits against the company.

This view of the termination process is admittedly one-sided and a bit unfair. Many executives care deeply about the people they are forced to fire. Outplacement counseling does give people a support system and skills to better manage a traumatic transition in their lives. The process becomes manipulative when it is done either as a public relations effort or a strategy to avoid a lawsuit.

Most of these activities have to do with the sharing and withholding of information. How much do we disclose, how soon, and to whom. As middle managers, we are constantly meeting with our peers, struggling to decide whether we should

- tell our subordinates where they really stand with us,

- tell those two levels above us about difficulties, disappointments, or doubts,

- communicate to the organization information about a deteriorating situation,

- let others know our real position on controversial business issues — especially in meetings of more than three people.

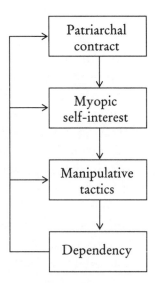

Figure 2.
Bureaucratic Cycle.

The process of selectively communicating these difficult issues with the intent of controlling the responses of others is the way we almost instinctively manipulate our environment.

The forms of manipulation described here are not in and of themselves cardinal sins. Rather, they are habitual ways we have learned to deal with each other in our attempt to adapt to the demands organizational life places on us. The price we pay for manipulative strategies is both personal and organizational. If we felt we had free choice, most of us would drop political behavior in favor of a more honest and direct approach. The fact that we feel it is necessary to be political/manipulative in order to succeed means that in the service of our ambition we have given away a part of ourselves. We shave off a thin slice of our own integrity in the name of effectiveness and practicality. Organizationally, manipulation creates dependency and caution in those around us. We want others to be entrepreneurial and autonomous, yet when we shade reality and treat them either as children or aliens, what we get back is more negative politics and bureaucracy.

The cumulative effect of this cycle gives life to negative politics and bureaucratic spirit (Figure 2). To transform organizations into places in which positive politics becomes the norm requires that we create an alternative, entrepreneurial cycle. In creating the alternative, we need to reexamine each element. We cannot try to stop being manipulative and still sign the patriarchal contract or define self-interest as getting ahead. It is too much to ask. The remainder of this book is dedicated to turning each of these elements around. The promise is not only to better serve the organization but also to claim our integrity, find new meaning in our work, and ground our self-esteem in something more permanent than overhangs and corner offices.

THREE

DEVELOPING ANTIDOTES

FOR BUREAUCRACY

Politics is the pursuit of power, and power is both a function of position in the hierarchy and, more importantly, a state of mind. The conventional wisdom is that if you want to change a way of doing business, you either have to be at the top or have angels at the top. There is no question that if the top executives support your efforts, life is easier than if they don't. But the power of position is overrated. We frequently find people near or at the top feeling as powerless as people at the middle or the bottom. We are reluctant to believe this because of our deep wish for our leaders to be powerful. Wishing for strong leadership doesn't make it so. Those at the top feel as caught in the middle as the rest of us.

I discovered this discouraging reality in working with First National Stores, a supermarket chain in the Northeast. First National, called Finast, was a dominant food chain in the forties and fifties, but in the early sixties, it was slow to react to competition from smaller chains with stores twice the size and with twice the weekly volume of Finast. A Finast store was averaging $40,000 in sales a week, while the newer chains such as Stop-N-Shop, Star Markets, and what is now known as Pathmark were averaging $100,000 a week, with some stores reaching an amazing $250,000 a week. They did this with larger stores, cut-rate prices, low service and labor cost, and aggressive neighborhood merchandising. Finast woke up to the dilemma in the early sixties and decided it needed to change its way of doing business. One of the keys to the change was to push more of the merchandising decisions closer to the store level and to begin to develop stronger store managers. The store manager traditionally had been more like a store supervisor, concerned primarily with labor scheduling, housekeeping, and executing orders from division headquarters, which came in the form of a twenty-page mimeographed document itemizing the pricing and merchandising plan for the week. Members of my firm were part of a consulting team brought in to change this process and help shift power to the store manager. Over the following year a variety of things were attempted to help the store managers take on their new role. Job descriptions were rewritten, incentive compensation systems based on store sales and profitability were introduced, college graduates were hired into the job with promises of bright futures, an extensive store manager training program was introduced, and communication meetings to explain the new role were held at all levels. These efforts began to make a dent in the role of some of the store managers, but the process was happening very slowly. In assessing why the change was happening so slowly, the common complaint was that we could not expect the store managers to change their role without the active day-to-day support of the managers above them. The district managers who supervised the store managers had the reputation of being rather autocratic and unwilling to give up control.

Understanding that one has to start at the top, our consulting team began a six-month program of redefining roles, redoing pay systems, and conducting participative management training for the district managers. This too seemed to move very slowly. Prior to our training and change effort, the district managers gave the store managers their marching orders as soon as they walked into the store, even before removing their hat and coat. We were telling the district managers to be more collaborative and deal with the store managers more as equals. They interpreted this mandate on a day-to-day basis by walking into a store, going to the store manager's office, and then removing their hat and coat before they gave the store manager the marching orders. At the end of the six months we once again assessed our impact and were told that the slow progress was due to the division managers, the people whom the district managers report to; they were the problem—they were the ones unwilling to give up any control.

Understanding that change has to start at the top, we began a three-month program of working with the division managers, most of whom were vice presidents. We did team building with the division managers and their staffs, we got the most autocratic ones reassigned, and we experimented with a leaner structure to push decision making down to the level of the store manager. As a result we continued to see some progress, but it was still too slow and at the end of three months we had a strategy meeting to decide what to do to speed up the change. One of our conclusions was that since we had spent a year with the store managers, six months with the district managers, and only three months with the division managers, at least it was taking us less and less time not to make progress at a given level. Another of our conclusions was that since one has to start at the top, it was time to schedule a meeting with the president of the company, Hilliard Coan. The president had sanctioned and financed everything that we had done to this point, but he had never really been the target of the change effort. His own actions had not yet come under our scrutiny. Hilly Coan was a powerful man, one of the most respected leaders in the industry. He had been brought in specifically to turn this supermarket chain around. We were confident that he, being at the top, must be the source of our problem and his conversion would be the source of our (and his) solution. We got on his calendar. I was to be the emissary of the change team.

I was especially eager for this meeting since it would be my first real opportunity to deal directly on an intimate basis with the person in the seat of power in a major corporation. Hilly

Coan had thirteen thousand employees and seven hundred stores reporting directly to him. After working with his company at every level for almost two years, I was prepared to have an intelligent conversation with him about his business and how he could use the power of his office and the power of his personal presence to make the changes he had initiated become a reality. If change had to come from the top, I was meeting with the right person.

The meeting was scheduled, and I arrived eager and dressed in my newly pressed power suit. After a little light chatter about the weather and the ball scores, I mentioned that the purpose of this meeting was to talk about how he could personally support the change effort we were engaged in. He said he had met with the chairman of the board of directors earlier that morning and the chairman brought up a series of minor issues that were a real nuisance to have to deal with. I suggested perhaps Hilliard, the president, could support our program more by personally getting out in the stores more. Hilliard said that the chairman was not giving him all the support he needed. I urged that Hilliard could perhaps allow certain merchandising decisions to be made at the district level instead of at the headquarters office in Somerville, Massachusetts. He said he was also having a hard time with certain analysts on Wall Street. They refused to acknowledge the progress the new management was making, and the stock price remained depressed. I suggested we might hold a team-building session with the top thirty people. He stated that not only were the chairman of the board and the bankers giving him a hard time, but he was frustrated with the ketchup in the company cafeteria.

It was at this point that I began to recognize that the conversation was not going the way that I had anticipated. I asked him to tell me a little more about the ketchup in the company cafeteria. He said it was too thin and watery. I acknowledged that watery ketchup could be deeply disappointing, thinking to myself that I had just stepped onto the set of a Woody Allen movie. Hilliard began to get a little irritated with me and claimed I did not understand the point that he was making. He was right. I noticed that he was wearing shoes with a clay-colored tint to them. He explained that the ketchup in the company cafeteria was a Finast private label brand, and two weeks ago he had suggested that the product needed to be thickened to compete effectively with the name brand products. He was constantly amazed at the effort it took to bring about even the smallest change in this old-line company. He thought that at least someone could have thickened the ketchup at his table in the company cafeteria, even if the product on the shelves remained watery.

I was stunned. I had thought that the president of a company could have it any way he or she wanted it. I had pursued the source of power all the way up the organization, and here the chief executive officer was telling me he was caught in the middle like the rest of us. He found it difficult to please those above him, and giving orders to those below him provided no guarantee that action would be taken. The meeting with Hilliard eventually got back on track. After some discussion, he agreed to get more personally involved and to reassess the level at which merchandising decisions were made, and we did have a team-building session with his people. As a postscript, Finast after a very sluggish beginning did move to larger, more store manager driven stores, but the effort was too late and the company was bought out by another chain.

The experience with the supermarket chain, brought to a head and symbolized by the discussion with the president about ketchup, demonstrated some important things about power and empowerment.

1. Even people at the top are in the middle. There is no absolute authority in an organization. We can talk as if the boss is in control, but it is more a wish than a reality.

2. Change from the top down happens at the will and whim of those below. As managers we state our intentions and give direction, but many of the most critical choices are made by the people below us.

3. The power of a boss is asymmetrical. It is easier to use authority to tighten up, shrink, and make an organization more cautious than it is to use power to open up, expand, and make an organization more courageous. There is a readiness of people in low-power positions to believe the worst. If it is fear that we want to instill in our subordinates, they are quite ready to respond. If on the other hand we want them to take more responsibility and be political in a positive way, that is so difficult it is worth writing a book about.

What this means is that empowerment is a state of mind as well as a result of position, policies, and practices. As managers we become more powerful as we nurture the power of those below us. One way we nurture those below us is by becoming a role model for how we want them to function. This begins when we create an entrepreneurial cycle within our own unit, whether our unit is the whole organization or a programming section buried in the basement of an administrative services division.

The entrepreneurial cycle is the antidote to the bureaucratic cycle. If left unattended, the bureaucratic cycle reinforces itself and encourages politics as usual. Operating in a bureaucratic culture increases the tendency to experience ourselves as vulnerable, losing control, and somewhat helpless.

- *Vulnerable.* Since cards are not on the table and communication is indirect, we never know what forces are going to come down on us. The rules are not explained to us because they shift and are difficult to justify.

- *Losing control.* Driven by a patriarchal, top-down contract, control is a sometime thing. It becomes an issue at every meeting; it is sought at every level. If we were not afraid of losing control so constantly, why would we have to seek it so vigorously?

- *Somewhat helpless.* While we might prefer the choice for greatness, courage, and autonomy, we find ourselves often choosing the opposite. Caution and dependency grow out of the belief that any other alternative would threaten our survival. As a result we engage in bureaucratic behavior as a defensive strategy.

Experiencing vulnerability, low control, and helplessness is the antithesis of being entrepreneurial and political in a positive way. If we allow ourselves to be controlled by the bureaucratic environment we may find ourselves in, we tend to operate in a low-trust way. We say yes when we mean no. We withhold information, we manage relationships toward our own ends, and we use language that smooths over reality. In functioning this way we are helping to create the very way of operating that we are defending ourselves against. The fact that this behavior works only intensifies our deeper sense of entrapment.

The way through this dilemma is to act in a way that serves our empowerment. Empowerment stems from two sources: (1) the structure, practices, and policies we support as managers who have control over others, and (2) the personal choices we make that are expressed by our own actions.

In examining the entrepreneurial cycle, each element of the cycle requires both personal choices about how we want to do business and opportunities through structure, process, and policy to support positive political behavior on the part of others. To feel empowered means several things.

- *We feel our survival is in our own hands.* Easy to say, difficult to do. It requires that we in every sense take responsibility for our situation. No one to blame, no matter what the circumstance; we are the ones who have essentially put it all together.

- *We have an underlying purpose.* Work is something more than paying the mortgage. Granted, we work because we have to, but if we are going to put in time, we have a goal or vision of something worthwhile. It may have to do with the product or service we deal with; it may have to do with the kind of organization we wish to create, or simply how we treat the people around us. It may take us years to know what our purpose is, but to be empowered, we have to believe it is in there somewhere.

- *We commit ourselves to achieving that purpose, now.* Knowing what we want to do and committing to do it are two separate acts. The act of commitment is to decide to fulfill the purpose of this job and not wait until conditions are more supportive. The commitment needs to be made regardless of who our boss is, or how the business is going, or how alone we seem to be in our purpose.

As managers, our task is to empower ourselves and to create conditions under which others can do the same. The entrepreneurial cycle serves us in this effort (Figure 3). Without restructuring our contract with the organization, our definition of self-interest, and our way of being political, our chances of finding our way out of the bureaucracy are slim.

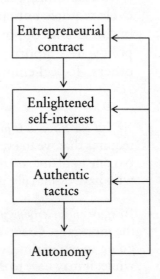

Figure 3.
Entrepreneurial Cycle.

To create an entrepreneurial cycle, it is necessary to renegotiate the essential contract between the person and the organization. Whereas the patriarchal contract requires us (1) to submit to authority, (2) to deny self-expression, and (3) to make sacrifices for unnamed future rewards, the entrepreneurial contract takes the other side. It requires us to

- be our own authority,

- encourage self-expression,

- make commitments,

- believe that the above are just.

BE OUR OWN AUTHORITY.   The first tenet of the patriarchal contract—that people need to submit to authority—places the focus of control outside the individual. The belief is that there is an external authority that demands top priority. The authority and the basis for action and decisions come from someone else, and that someone else is always at a higher level. This tenet needs to be reexamined and renegotiated. This mind-set has the opposite effect of what we as managers want. Our most valued subordinates are those who take most responsibility for the unit.

If we ask people to take responsibility for their own actions and their own unit and to create an organization of their own choosing, there's no choice but to adopt the belief that authority comes from within. Our basic contract is that the employees are the ultimate source of authority on what actions will best serve this business. This means that we as managers have to give up some of our control, deemphasize the power we have over people under us, and acknowledge that while the captain may choose direction, the engine room drives the ship.

Although we may give up some control, to follow this path is not to give up structure or different levels in the hierarchy. The pyramid still functions in a positive way to keep us focused on purpose and goals and to give us some structure within which to operate. The contract between the employee and the organization in effect states that the employees are responsible for their own actions and the success of their unit or their project. We should no longer give such emphasis to the need to submit to authority. We should instead demand that people are here to make their own choices about what's best for this business.

If we are serious about contracting for internal authority, here are some things we might do.

1. *If we want to begin with a radical act, show the organization with the pyramid turned upside down.* Put the people at the lowest level of your unit at the top; put yourself at the bottom (Figure 4).

The president of SAS airlines does this. He is at the bottom of the pyramid, and the reservations and customer service people are at the top. The concept expresses the intent that management's primary purpose is to support the people who support the customer.

2. *If turning the organization upside down is too big a leap, flatten it out.* The extreme example of a bureaucratic organization

Figure 4.
Inverted Pyramid.

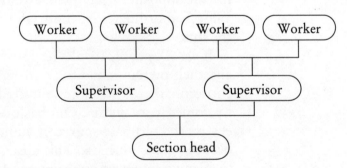

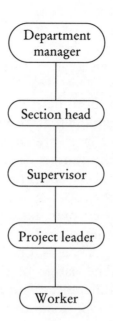

Figure 5.
Top-Heavy Structure.

would be to have a series of levels with each person having one subordinate (Figure 5). A way to communicate that the success of the organization rests on each person's shoulders is to create a flat structure. Instead of a pyramid, use a pancake as the model for the unit (Figure 6).

Returning for a moment to the effort at First National Stores, we finally decided that no amount of training or job redefinition would get the district manager off of the store manager's back. Instead, the company gave each district manager forty stores rather than the usual thirteen. With thirteen stores, the district manager was physically able to visit each

Figure 6.
Pancake Structure.

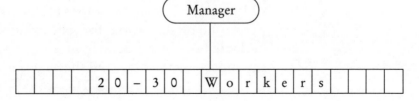

store one or two times a week. With forty stores, the district manager could visit fifteen stores a week. That left at least twenty-five stores free to manage themselves each week.

Each organization has its own mythology about how many subordinates one supervisor can manage. Generally, fifteen to eighteen is thought to be too many subordinates. Most sources estimate that five to eight may be about right. Limiting the number of subordinates makes sense only if the job of the supervisor is primarily to maintain control. When the job of the superior is to push control down so that people become their own authority, who knows what the limits of span of control are?

There is, of course, a limit to how flat the pancake can be. The nature of the task being performed does make a big difference. More complex, technical, and volatile jobs need the support and teaching that a smaller group and greater supervisory involvement can provide. Also, when supervision is taken away, a greater investment in the development of the subordinates needs to be made. The point, however, is to let the organization structure express our intention to demand that people act on their own internal authority.

3. Change the ground rules about when a supervisor supervises. Let the role of the supervisor be consultative and by invitation only. The subordinates decide when to involve their supervisor. To the supervisor, this may feel like anarchy, but if a subordinate has clear goals and accountability, it has worked. It is another way to affirm that authority comes from within.

4. Reverse the performance appraisal process. It's not easy to play God, so why not stop trying. Let each person be responsible for conducting two appraisals: his or her own and the person he or she works for. For example, as a subordinate I evaluate how I have done in meeting my goals and also assess my supervisor on how well she has done in supporting me and in reaching her own goals. This would serve to balance out the power a little bit and express the belief that I and my supervisor have a common interest in each other's success.

5. *Introduce self-managing teams.* Self-managing teams are being tried in many places, mostly in manufacturing, with great success.[3] Basically the team, not the supervisor, is responsible for the recruiting, selection, scheduling, assignments, equipment purchases, and quality control. The supervisor, whose title is sometimes changed to area manager, is responsible for defining output requirements and negotiating with the rest of the organization for the resources the team needs.

6. *Encourage subordinates to call meetings.* Staff meetings are the family dinner of organizational life. They have symbolic significance because they may be the only time that everyone in the unit is in a room together. The norms and process of the staff meeting influence our attitude about the unit to a far greater extent than simply the subject matter at hand. Let the convening, structuring, and managing of the staff meeting be everyone's responsibility.

7. *See that assignments become a two-way contract.* Traditionally, assignments are given by the boss; the subordinates ask questions for clarification, and off they go to do the work. In this process the wants of only one of the parties, the boss, are being expressed. Work is done most effectively through social contracts in which the wants of both parties get expressed. An entrepreneurial contract concerning assignments would have the supervisor say, "Here is what I want from you; now tell me what you want from me." Simple — but it captures the spirit.

The number of actions that would express the intention that

---

[3] E. E. Lawler, *High-Involvement Management* (San Francisco: Jossey-Bass, 1986).

if people respond to their internal authority it is good for the business is endless. Most of us are in some ways already working in that direction. Ideally we want this intention to run throughout everything that we do. Too often we treat people as partners in the morning but turn around and treat them as children in the afternoon.

ENCOURAGE SELF-EXPRESSION.   The second element of an entrepreneurial contract has to do with self-restraint and self-expression. As mentioned earlier, the patriarchal belief is that self-restraint is essential to building a strong organization. How people feel doesn't matter. We're not here to run a sensitivity group; this is not a place for touchy/feely stuff. Feelings and subjectivity have no place in the rational, scientific world of organizational life.

The price we pay for this attitude is that we put a cap on the well of people's motivation and passion and caring about the organization. The reality is that all business is personal and people care deeply about their jobs and the other people around them. We all need to feel supported in our self-expression, in trusting our intuition, and in accepting the emotional side of our existence. When we deny self-expression, systems tend to be flat, gray, lacking in passion and excitement. Denial creates boredom, repetition, and bureaucracy.

An entrepreneurial organization is designed to create the opposite, a setting in which people put passion, energy, excitement, and motivation into their work. More times than we'd like to admit, managers talk about lighting a fire under their employees. They stand by their windows late in the day and they complain that everybody is leaving the office at quitting time. People's desire to leave at quitting time, their desire to take long breaks and long lunches, and their desire to fulfill themselves outside the job are a direct consequence of an anti-self-expression culture, philosophy, and contract. It is only the bureaucrat who has no feelings, makes no exceptions, does everything by the book, follows the rules, and lives a life of total predictability. The objectivity and rationality we yearn for in organizations is only partially obtainable. Organizations are too complicated to be totally predictable and to operate on plan. What we want is people who can adapt to unpredictable situations, to the nonroutine, to unique demands of their customers, and to react with energy and motivation and the organization's interest at heart. This requires access to intuition. It requires listening to how people are feeling about what they're doing.

To put into words how we feel about what's happening at work with regard to projects and people is an act of taking responsibility for who we are, what we stand for, and our own experience. There is no point at which people take more responsibility for their lives and their actions than when they put into words their own wants and their own feelings. Those two issues are at the center of motivation, at the center of responsibility, focus, and action. There is nothing a manager can do to support an entrepreneurial attitude with more impact than simply to ask people two questions: "What do you want?" and "How are you feeling?" These both respond to people's need to feel that their actions are critical to our success.

The fear we have of encouraging self-expression is that ultimately the organization will become one large therapy group. People will spend their time simply talking about how they feel without really committing themselves to positive action. When we go from a culture that supports no self-expression to one that supports high self-expression there will be a bumpy transition period. There is no question that after being denied expression, people will overdo the time and energy spent in talking about feelings, intuition, and the subjective parts of their work. The price we pay for encouraging self-expression is lower short-term efficiency. It takes more time; it seems on the surface less focused and controlled. The payoff for encouraging self-expression is the level of motivation, energy, and commitment that we get from each person.

Another frustration in encouraging self-expression is that when we ask people how they are feeling, many of them don't know. Our culture, our upbringing, our family have so encouraged the suppression of feelings, especially for men, that if we say to some people, "How do you feel?" the answer is—silence. Or we get back a series of intellectualized ideas about what they think is happening outside themselves. One of the unique qualities women have to offer an organization is their general facility in knowing and articulating their own feelings and experience. Growing up female (so I've been told) means being supported in exploring the intuitive and emotional side of life. Most organizational cultures view this as a weakness, and many women think they have to suppress their feelings at work in order to be accepted and seen as powerful. We should be viewing access to feelings as a corporate asset and support it in all employees.

There is inevitably a period of struggle, and in some cases of failure, in asking an organization to support self-expression as a way of doing business. No system is going to work for all people, so why not create a culture that supports the best of what we want from people rather than creating a culture that responds to those people who under any circumstances would be unable to give us what we want.

Developing actions that encourage self-expression is a little more intangible than creating ways to push authority inside the person. Basically it requires a decision to ask people how they feel and the patience to listen to their response. This means we need to acknowledge the existence of their feelings without having to agree or disagree with them. It is difficult to listen to people who work for us express frustrations about things when those frustrations are not what we intended and are so different from our own experience. We just have to keep telling ourselves not to take it personally and that there is nothing to defend. In addition to asking people how they feel and listening better, we could take other steps to reinforce the self-expression element of the contract.

1. Devote 25 percent of each meeting to issues of attitude, morale, and motivation.   Often we have the intention of using a portion of meetings to discuss how things are going, but we put it last on the agenda and never really get to it. So do it first. A simple structure for encouraging expression is to ask the people attending the meeting to think over the last two months and identify things that have made them proud and things that they are sorry about. The goal is to bring these discussions out of the bathrooms, car pools, cocktail lounges, and lunchrooms and into the meetings and "business" discussions. Doing this both legitimizes self-expression and ensures that the right people are in the room to hear.

2. Try a do-it-yourself attitude survey. The most common method of examining feelings is through an attitude survey. While such surveys can be useful for bringing feelings to the surface, they have some limitations when used in traditional ways. Surveys are traditionally taken by either third-party interviews or questionnaires. Questionnaire results are comforting because they have numbers. Numbers give the illusion of objectivity and measurement. Third-party interviews have similar benefits, but the problem with both is that it is hard to know how to act on the results. At best, third-party surveys form the basis for a useful discussion between boss and subordinate. Why not simply have the discussion to begin with by asking the supervisors to do the interviews themselves. The argument against this is that you lose confidentiality. But that is the very purpose of the survey — to eliminate the need for secrecy and caution. The first or second time you ask your subordinates how things are going, they might not trust you enough to give an honest answer, but if you keep asking, eventually they will believe that you want to hear and tell you. The whole idea is to make these more intimate and personal conversations a normal way of doing business and not a special once-a-year thing.

These simple steps may seem a far distance from the hard-nosed political skills you might have picked this book out for, but they are political acts because they go against the culture that most of us are accustomed to. They are acts of advocacy for an alternative to the patriarchal contract. Supporting self-expression is a way of creating a self-correcting mechanism against actions that occur but are not in the best interest of the people or the organization. Too often, ill-advised projects or practices continue because of a community of silence. People have doubts about a project, but think that they are the only ones who have those doubts and amidst the silence defer to the seeming confidence of others. Encouraging the expression of feelings is also a way of letting your people know that the messenger may be frowned at, but will not be shot.

MAKE COMMITMENTS.   The third element of the entrepreneurial contract is to demand commitment instead of sacrifice. To make a commitment to something is to say, "I'm going to do what I believe in, what I want to do, and I commit to doing it out of my own choice." We too often make sacrifices in response to external demands and justify our actions by the statement that we have to. The essence of a contract of sacrifice is to do what we are obligated to do and constant use of the words *have to*.

The alternative is to talk about what we want to do. When we ask people to make choices, to take responsibility for their actions, they are required to state their own wants. We ask for no favors, no sacrifice. To ask for a favor is to say, "I want you to do something I know you don't want to do, but please do it for my sake." We are asking at that moment for others to base their actions on external motivation. This leads to the dependent mind-set. To create an organization that values autonomy, we ask people to choose, to express their wants directly and simply. We ask them to make commitments to what they're doing, and we say that if this is not something they want to do, then we need to keep talking about it.

Committing ourselves and doing what we want to do is not an act of self-indulgence. Again, we have to believe that people care about the organization, they're committed to its goals and purpose, and their deepest wish is to contribute something meaningful. If we believe our employees want this organization to succeed, there is no reason to believe that asking them to commit to how they want to proceed would encourage a self-indulgent or antiorganizational direction.

There is no question that people do work for a living and there are times we have to do things that we would rather not do, but it is still possible for us to make the choice and make the commitment to engage in unpleasant, boring, routine, or painful tasks because we know they are there for a good purpose and serve a larger goal. The fear we have in giving up sacrifice and encouraging people to do what they're committed to do is that people will go off in every direction and will not hold the organization's interest at heart. This, again, is a pessimistic view of human nature.

If we were at all optimistic, we would ask people seriously to think about what they wanted to commit to. An internally generated act of choice and commitment results in people's feeling much more responsible for outcomes. There is no pressure more powerful than that which comes from within. Our task as managers is to encourage people to make demands on themselves.

The other price we pay for demanding sacrifices is that when we sacrifice we expect something in return. An act of sacrifice creates obligations on the manager that then become a hidden bargain. The statement is "I'll sacrifice for you now, but you better take care of me later." Resentment runs deep in the person who has made a sacrifice when he or she realizes at a later date that the sacrifice was supposed to have been made for its own sake and its own reward. When we ask people to make commitments and to choose, they do it for the present. No hidden bargains, no obligations. The act of making a commitment gives meaning to what people are doing. A commitment provides its own reward. Unless you are a masochist, sacrifice depends on a later reward that often never comes.

The entrepreneurial choice, at its center, is a choice for risk and to bet the farm. There is no way in the world that a person acting out of a sense of duty and sacrifice will find the strength to take the risky path. The only justification for taking a risk and creating an organization of your own choosing is to do it out of a commitment to something you believe in. In a sense, something that you have to do. The "have to do" comes from inside, not outside. Asking people to take risks on the basis that it's their duty, or is good for some people other than themselves, is asking too much, and it doesn't work.

The reason that people leave the office at exactly five o'clock, lobby for longer coffee breaks, and negotiate for more pay for less hours is because they're viewing their work as an act of sacrifice and obligation, something that's being done to pay the mortgage. The reason they want to leave right on time is because they see their evenings and weekends as the place for autonomy, self-expression, and personal commitment. Our task as managers is to bring those qualities into the workday.

Self-expression is served by asking people how they feel; commitment is served by asking people what they want. Stating what we want is the essential act of taking responsibility. Our goal as managers is to achieve a fifty-fifty sense of responsibility for the success of our unit. Commitment comes when we feel ourselves grow, out of our own choice. Stating our wants, taking responsibility, committing ourselves, this is how we overcome a sense of helplessness. Often we do not get what we want, but in a sense it doesn't matter. Helplessness and low-energy sacrifice come from the unfinished business of not having taken a stance and made the statement of what we wanted. We empower ourselves and those around us by compulsively asking the question "If this is what we have to get done, what do you want from me and others to make it happen?"

Here are some specific things we can do to help replace sacrifice with commitment.

1. *At the simplest level, stay focused on what we and those around us want.* This is particularly helpful in meetings where a fog has settled over the discussion. Fog occurs when we get caught up in discussing the history, defending ourselves, blaming others, and getting too involved in details. Asking the ques-

tion "What do you want?" slices through the fog. If people do not know what they want, then ask the question "If you did know what you wanted, what would it be?"

2. Act in ways that give others ownership. We commit to that which we own. Sacrifice is a process of dis-owning. When we sacrifice we give up a part of ourselves, or disown ourselves. We create ownership/commitment when we

- give others freedom to choose their own path to achieving results,

- structure work so that people are doing a whole job instead of a piece of a job.

3. Discourage and confront passive, nonassertive behavior. Passive behavior is an extreme form of withholding. Passive people remain silent as a strategy for getting what they want. Passive behavior often has the effect of making us feel either guilty or sorry for quiet people. We have to keep reminding ourselves that passivity is political, a goal-seeking stance, and that other people are nowhere near as vulnerable as they appear.

4. Create a vision of greatness for ourselves and ask our subordinates to do the same. Creating a vision of greatness will be dealt with in a later chapter, but we claim ownership over our lives when we identify the future that we want for ourselves and our unit. Our deepest commitment is to choose to live, to choose the destiny that has been handed to us, and to choose to pursue that destiny. These choices are expressed at work when we create a vision for our unit and decide to pursue that vision at all costs.

In a sense, this list of steps doesn't do justice to the issue of commitment. In fact, building ownership or commitment is what this whole book is about. The steps do, however, present clues regarding where to put our attention as we try to combat the attitude of sacrifice that we see growing out of the patriarchal contract we are trying to change.

BELIEVE THAT THE ABOVE ARE JUST.   Believing that the above are just, the final element of an entrepreneurial contract is to believe that real authority comes from within and that self-expression and commitment are good for the business. We decide to build an organization based on this optimistic view. The belief, outlined earlier under the patriarchal contract, that strong external authority, self-denial, and sacrifice are good for the business is a more pessimistic view of human nature. Which view we take is really a choice each of us individually makes since there is plenty of evidence to support both positions. Evil does exist in the world, and people, including ourselves, often do choose personal gain over what is good for the community. At the same time, we have the experience of seeing people choose what is good for the organization, even at their own expense. We adopt a view of what is possible on the basis of our own free will, not because someone forces us. Given the ambiguity of external data, why not create an entrepreneurial contract with our employees. We will pay a price for yielding some authority, listening to feelings, and coping with what people want to do, but we pay a price for any contract we negotiate.

Many of us are quite willing to give entrepreneurial choice to our top performers. We give them more authority, self-expression, and freedom. We expect less from our average performers, and that is what we get. Demanding that each employee take responsibility for the business would, over time, create a culture of high performers. The entrepreneurial contract makes very difficult demands on people, demands that bureaucratic employees will find hard to live with. People who do not want to take responsibility will find ways to avoid it, but let them find that somewhere else. If we want to choose a bureaucratic path and be political in the traditional way, there are lots of places to go. It takes an act of faith for us to decide that it is possible for us to create a unique culture in our own unit. The starting point for that is to think through the basic nature of our contract with our people.

The next step is to determine how we want to define self-interest for ourselves and our unit. Self-interest is at the center of how we choose to be political and is discussed in the following section.

ENLIGHTENED SELF-INTEREST

When we define self-interest as the pursuit of safety, control, advancement, approval, and territory for its own sake, the bureaucratic way of operating is almost inevitable. Negative politics is created when I feel the organization in some way owns me and leads me to believe that moving ahead in the organization is good for me and helpful to my self-esteem. If my primary vehicle for feeling empowered is to move up the ladder in a system that offers little autonomy, I am forced to operate in manipulative ways. Once again, manipulation is attempting to influence others without letting them know we are doing it.

All of us have a wish to be more authentic and non-manipulative in the way that we operate, but we're not sure that we can be successful along that path. We see the manipulation taking place around us; in fact, it's so ingrained in organizational cultures that sometimes we hardly know we're doing it. Our dominant wish early in our career is to get even better at manipulation, which is called being politically sophisticated. We seek to know the rules and want to learn how to live by them. We are grateful when we have a supervisor who is skillful at navigating the corridors of the organization. Our ultimate rationalization is that manipulation works—and it does work.

To break the cycle that results in manipulation requires that we reorder the way we view our self-interest. It is necessary to give secondary priority to the personal, career-advancing self-interest that we typically have and to develop the mind-set that our primary self-interest is inevitably linked and interdependent with the self-interest of the business and the other people around us. The major purpose of our work is to build an organization of our own choosing and one that we believe in. We live at risk if we move up through the organization in a way that we have doubts about. We can rationalize our actions with the belief that it will be different when we achieve a higher level or more responsibility. The risk is that we have undermined our major purpose. It is possible to be personally "successful" but in the process to lose a part of ourselves while we support an environment that we really would like to change. Therefore, how we get ahead is as critical as how far we go.

Genuine, long-term self-interest, though typically defined as doing those things that will get us to the top, is better served if we act first and foremost to serve the organization and make our own personal ascension the second priority. This is not an issue of morality but a practical path to empowerment. Being driven to serve the organization is the essence of enlightened self-interest. It is also at the heart of positive politics. Enlightened self-interest involves several pursuits.

ENLIGHTENED SELF-INTEREST NO. 1: MEANING.   We decide that we will engage in activities that have meaning to us and are genuinely needed. Our unit does those things that express our values about what we have to contribute to the organization. We stop engaging in activities designed to defend ourselves, to explain ourselves, and to go into the history of how we got here. We minimize efforts designed to control people who are controlling others, efforts designed to position and reposition, to promote, and to rationalize. No more dry runs, dress rehearsals, and detailed strategies on whom to meet with and when. All activities that are synonymous with the protective, careful, cautious culture of bureaucratic environment we decide not to engage in. We cast our fate to the wind and do the things that have meaning and depth and substance for our unit, even if we think they may not win approval or blessings from those around us. We commit to the pursuit of substance over form.

ENLIGHTENED SELF-INTEREST NO. 2: CONTRIBUTION AND SERVICE. We decide to do the things that we feel genuinely contribute to the organization and its purpose. Each unit has its own unique contribution to make to the business, and the people in it have their own unique contributions to make to the unit. Our self-interest is best served when we're focused on contributing the things that are of unique value to the business. If they do not serve the business, if they do not serve the users and customers of our department, then we decide not to do them. No more "make work" projects, no more committees studying committees on oversight. We focus on a service orientation, giving away everything we have to give and holding onto as little as possible. When it comes to information, we want to share as much information as possible, and if we have to decide whether to act in a way that makes our own unit look good as opposed to another unit, we choose to make the other unit look good.

We treat this business as if it were our own. If it were our own business, we would not want rivalry, competition, and undermining actions to take place among the units working for us. If it were our own business, we wouldn't want people doing things just to look good; we would want people doing things because they had meaning for the business and served their users. The service orientation treats the other units inside the business as our customers, and we don't mess around with our customers for long. In many organizations other units are treated as adversaries. For example, typically, the research organization sees marketing and manufacturing as being somewhat unreasonable and difficult to deal with. Marketing people see manufacturing and research in rather negative terms. They see manufacturing as inflexible and unresponsive. Marketing sees research as taking too long and being self-indulgent in its wish for excellence, elegance, and discovery. Manufacturing in turn thinks research does not know how to design a product at a reasonable cost and in a predictable way. Manufacturing tends to see marketing as being wishy-washy, unable either to make up its mind or to hold onto a position long enough to be profitable.

All of these attitudes are common in every organization and to some extent inevitable. We want a certain amount of tension between organizations—we want them to see the world in different ways. Each function is an advocate for the integrity of its own activity, and that has to lead to some amount of conflict. Underneath conflict, though, we need the orientation that each unit is there to serve the others. Marketing in a sense becomes the customer of manufacturing and research. Research sees manufacturing and marketing as its customers and has the orientation that it exists to serve its customers and contribute something unique to them. Seeing other units as our customers forces us to give priority to their requirements. When we focus on contribution and service, it allows us to let go of the struggles for control and territory that are so common.

The greatest frustration of living inside a bureaucratic organization is that we can see no clear path to contributing something of real value to the organization.

ENLIGHTENED SELF-INTEREST NO. 3: INTEGRITY.   All of us have the fear, conscious or unconscious, that we cannot maintain our integrity and still move up in the organization and be successful. We have the feeling that if we stand up, we'll be shot. There is a widespread belief that if we deliver bad news, it will be our last act and that what was true for the Greeks will be true for us—people shoot the messenger.

To maintain our integrity in the organization essentially means to put into words what we see happening, to tell people what is really going on within our unit and what we see going on outside our unit. Integrity isn't a moral issue; it's not a question of fraud or legally dishonest acts. It is more the issue of whether it is possible for us to tell the truth about what we see happening, to make only those promises that we can deliver on, to admit to our mistakes, and to have the feeling that the authentic act is always the best for the business.

Acting with integrity goes against a myth that dominates organizations. Every organization has a story about someone who stood up and was shot, of some individual who took a strong stand in line with his own beliefs and was destroyed for the act of taking that stand. Try to research who the person was, what the stand was, when the event happened, who shot the person. Often it's very hard to find out these things. The person who got shot somehow is unnameable, the event always happened four or five years ago, nobody that you talk to was actually in the room. But the conviction remains that around this place, if you stand up and tell people what's really going on, you'll be shot.

The irony is that the generals are as imprisoned by the myth as the soldiers. As a manager, it's very hard to find out exactly what's going on. You get so many different stories you never know what the truth is, and when people report to you on projects and events, you're never sure whether they're describing what's really happening or whether they're positioning their statements to you in a way that proclaims their own innocence.

When we choose integrity as absolutely being in our self-interest, we go against the myths about the slain bodies of our comrades. This does not mean that choosing integrity brings a guarantee of safe passage. People do get fired. This book began with the story of Allan, who had seemingly successfully created an entrepreneurial division in the midst of a bureaucratic environment. He had essentially met his sales and profit goals and yet found himself unexpectedly on the job market. At first glance it appears that his corporate deviance led to his demise. After talking at length with him and people around him it seems that it was the arrogance and aggressiveness with which he pursued his vision rather than the uniqueness of the vision itself that got him in trouble. Allan's strength was his courage and single-mindedness in pursuing his vision of an entrepreneurial organization. His vulnerability was his aggressive behavior and disdain for those who chose another path. The conventional stereotype of the entrepreneur is someone who will pursue a business opportunity with the heart of a champion but who has the interpersonal skills of a wild boar. We risk getting shot when we claim our integrity at the expense of others. We tell the world that we are taking a stand on something that we believe in, but we do it in a way that puts other people down. Our self-interest is best served when we hold onto our integrity and do it in a way that does not discount those around us.

The ultimate argument against the integrity of total honesty is that each of us knows someone who told the truth, did it in a nice way, and still got punished. That someone may even have been ourselves. The only answer to that is that Yes, Virginia, organizations are unfair. We do at times get punished for positive acts, but when that happens I always figure I was going to get punished no matter what I did. If I am going to get shot, the bullet probably left the gun some time ago and is already well on its way. If that is the case, I might as well act with integrity and go down in style.

ENLIGHTENED SELF-INTEREST NO. 4: POSITIVE IMPACT ON OTHERS' LIVES.   It is in our self-interest to treat other people well. All of us care deeply about the well-being of our colleagues and the people around us. Organizations for most of us are the primary meeting place. We each have strong personal values and often religious values about how other people are to be treated. There is something about a bureaucratic environment or a negatively political environment that allows us to suspend those beliefs in the name of getting something done. There is a great deal of conventional wisdom about not getting too close to the people around us because someday we may have to fire them. There is the belief that we don't want to say anything upsetting to our colleagues because someday we may have to work for them. Someday those people may work for us. There is the belief that if we get too close to other people, somehow it will hinder our ability to make objective decisions.

The connection is made between intimacy and openness with other people and weakness and subjectivity. The dominant fear is that if we get close to other people, it will ruin our objectivity, that we will make decisions designed to protect the intimacy of those relationships at the expense of the business.

All of these beliefs are rationalizations for treating people in ways that we don't feel comfortable about. They're based on a very narrow view of what's possible in organizations and what's possible in relationships. On the basis of the view that relationships tend to be rather brittle and are easily broken, there's no room for us to treat others honestly; according to this view, relationships in organizations, especially with the powerful people, have little forgiveness. To the contrary, confronting other people with the reality of what is happening is not an act of violence but an act of compassion. The way we treat people poorly in organizations is mostly by acts of omission and noncommunication. There is the feeling of withholding and caution that we justify by saying, "I don't want to hurt them." This, in fact, is an act of organizational cruelty. For other people not to know how we feel about their projects or their actions is a withholding, bureaucratic act.

To talk about third parties who are not in the room is not to treat those parties well. There is much more dialogue of a personal nature about people who are not in the room than actual direct communication. That's why performance reviews have been singularly unsuccessful over the years. They demand that, at an appointed hour, people have to really be direct and tell each other how they feel about performance and talk about how the organization feels about them. The depth and quality and intimacy of this conversation goes against the norms that dominate the other 364 days of the year. To ask people to behave this way once a year is asking too much.

The other dimension of having a positive impact on other people's lives has to do with the nature of the products and services that we're offering. As a function, we need to decide what services are of genuine value to other people and become a user- or customer-driven function. If the service or product of my unit is not one that I feel is genuinely helpful or has a positive effect on the people using it, then it's something that I should stop offering.

Auditing, policing, enforcing policy can be major forms of inflicting damage on other people in the organization. People in the staff role feel that top management is their real client. They work as the agents of top management in the name of their stewardship function. Staff people get involved in judging people, judging activities, making recommendations, and generally acting in a policing capacity. The policing is useful only to the extent that the people receiving the policing, the objects of scrutiny, are requesting that service. The only time auditing, policing, and evaluating treat people well and positively is when those being audited and policed actually request that kind of attention.

Auditors who move into an organization at the request of top management are really, in effect, letting their own top management off the hook. The staff-auditing or policy-enforcement group is doing the dirty work for the top management that wants to keep its hands clean. Much of the disservice done to other people is done in the name of top management or done in the name of what's good for the business. It is always a sign that what you are doing goes against your own beliefs when you hear yourself rationalizing it for the sake of someone or something that's not in the room.

ENLIGHTENED SELF-INTEREST NO. 5: MASTERY.   The final component of enlightened self-interest is the goal of simply learning as much as you can about the activity that you're engaged in. There's a pride and satisfaction in understanding your function better than anyone else and better than even you thought possible. One of the fastest ways to get out of a bureaucratic cycle is to have as your goal to learn as much as you can about what you're doing. Learning and performance are intimately related; the high performers are those who learn most quickly.

Performing a function simply for its own sake always serves

your best self-interest. To perform a function because it's dirty work that has to be done and somebody has to do it, is a sign that what you're doing may not be worth the effort. This final element of enlightened self-interest involves doing those things that would allow you to be the best and let that be its own reward. To learn something or perform something simply because somebody else wants you to do it is always a feeble motivation and marginally rewarding activity.

THE PAYOFF.   The powerful thing about enlightened self-interest is that it is a definition of self-interest that is under our control. To pursue mastery, meaning, contribution, integrity, service is to take a path that does not require the approval or applause of our supervisor. It is the only way to discover and claim our own autonomy, even in the midst of a dependency-creating organization. If I define self-interest only as those things that win the approval or are under the control of other people, I am dictating a dependent life-style for myself. Contribution, service, meaning, integrity, and touching other people in a positive way are all things I can do on my own.

Pursuing things independently of others' approval is the essence of the entrepreneurial spirit. To ask people to let go of their intense ambition to move up the organization with wider responsibility and more corporate jewelry is a fierce demand. There is nothing more difficult in the creation of an entrepreneurial or positively political organization than to ask people to let go of these historical, popular, and well-reinforced ambitions. The organization has designed a thousand ways to encourage people to define self-interest as moving up. The culture defines success in terms of status and trappings and jewelry and boats and trips and all the physical things that help us feel good about ourselves.

The literature of business has a strong implication that happiness is only found at the top. The business schools teach business only from the perspective of being the chief executive officer or the chief financial or marketing or personnel officer. The implication is that these are the only jobs that are really connected with success. In the name of creating an organization of our own choosing or being entrepreneurial, we ask people to turn at least sideways away from this definition of self-interest and to focus on their unit as if it's their own business. The down side of having your own business is that you have no place to go. There is no career development for people at the top of the organization. To be entrepreneurial in the midst of an organization is to proceed as if your career development is secondary and to stay focused on your product and service, and on the way it is delivered. This is a radical demand but one that's absolutely essential.

One of the problems with choosing enlightened self-interest over advancement is that it is a long-run strategy and we tend to live for today. The dominant norm of most organizations is to talk about the long run and act on the short run. To define self-interest as moving ahead is a short-run orientation, and organizations are filled with short runs. Actions that have long-run benefits are much less visible. To be entrepreneurial and political in a positive way means we have to feel we're in it for the long run. What we do for the short run, in fact, can guarantee a very short run. A short run is always used as a rationalization for doing something that we don't believe in.

One more argument in favor of enlightened self-interest. A dominant myth is that our career progression is directly linked with our performance. We all have the wish that if we perform well and live by the rules, we'll be acknowledged and rewarded. The real world is not so simple or direct. Our movement up through the organization, in reality, takes on much more of a random pattern than simply good reward for good performance. There are times when we're working very productively and nobody knows it and other times when we're limping along and are recognized. Our supervisors rotate every year or two, so we are constantly starting over, and who knows what our new boss will look for.

In addition, on a very practical level, medium- to large-sized organizations are getting smaller and smaller. Whole levels are being eliminated. The number of opportunities for promotion is shrinking. If we don't find alternatives to advancement as the measure of success, there are going to be a lot of frustrated middle-aged people.

AUTHENTIC TACTICS

Given a contract that supports autonomy, self-expression, and commitment plus a definition of self-interest focused on contribution, the next step is to identify tactics that are political and positive. Authentic acts are an antidote to the manipulative tactics outlined earlier. These actions are political because they are a way of advocating our self-interest—when our self-interest is defined as contribution, service, integrity, and treating people well. These actions also support an entrepreneurial mind-set because they demand we take complete responsibility for our own actions and the fortunes of our unit.

The fundamental strategy is to ensure that our unit is a model for how we want the whole organization to operate. All of us have a set of values that we want our organization to embody. We have a vision of a preferred future we wish for our unit. This vision includes how we want to work with our users and customers, how we want to operate within our unit, and the kind of quality standards we have for our product or service.

Others are influenced by how they see us act, so when our actions are aligned with the vision/preferred future we have for our unit, we have maximum political leverage. Too often, managers' own actions run contrary to their stated intentions about their product, service, or style. Incongruence between our actions and our promises undermines our credibility. Better for autocratic managers to acknowledge their wish for control than to try, unsuccessfully, to be participative.

Being a living example of our own vision also keeps us focused on the performance of our own unit rather than being distracted by worrying too much about those above us or other groups. We can't control how the rest of the organization operates; we do have some control over the group that reports to us. Getting our own house in order may not seem a global enough objective, but it is the most practical thing we can do.

To be more specific, here are some actions that will get rid of manipulation and move us toward a more entrepreneurial way of managing. We can take four basic approaches to avoid being manipulative and, instead, to be authentic in our transactions:

- say no when we mean no,

- share as much information as possible,

- use language that describes reality,

- avoid repositioning for the sake of acceptance.

SAY NO WHEN WE MEAN NO.   Instead of hedging our position for fear of being disapproved of, we make it a point to let others know where we stand. No more corporate fogging by "touching base," "running it up the flag pole," "requesting further study," or saying that something is a good idea, but the timing isn't right. No more committing to schedules we know we can't meet or promising a level of quality or cost that we know we cannot deliver. Most of us have a fear of saying no, thinking we might be seen as uncooperative or uncommitted. It is a risk we need to take. Too much money is wasted and too many expectations are violated when we are reluctant to take a stand early in a project. Our role models should be six-year-olds. They talk straight. They agree, they disagree, they like, they hate, they say yes, they say no. Period. After age six, our education, life experience, and general sophistication teach us to be cautious about communicating our real intent. If we feel that we cannot say no, then our yes's don't mean anything.

SHARE AS MUCH INFORMATION AS POSSIBLE.   Sharing as much information as possible is the opposite of the military notion that only those who "need to know" should be informed. Our goal is to let people know of our plans, ideas, changes as soon as possible. When we are thinking of reorganizing, we tell our people right away instead of waiting until the plan is fully formulated. If a project is running behind schedule, we tell our users we are behind. Most supervisors think part of their role is to shield their subordinates from bad news coming from above. When we shield our people we are acting as their parents and treating them like children. If we are trying to create the mind-set that everyone is responsible for the success of this business, then our people need complete information. We need to think of our subordinates and bosses as partners rather than as children or parents. Most of us know that if we withheld information from our partners, we would be putting the relationship at risk. Why not treat those above and below us, even our customers, the same way we would treat our partners? Sounds pretty reasonable and straightforward. If we really decide to act on this philosophy, here are some things we can start doing in a number of areas.

Financial Information

- Let everyone in the unit know what the budget looks like. Let the group see the breakdown by section and each of the line items. Tell them during the year how the unit is doing against the budget — even in areas outside their particular job.

- Make sales forecasts common knowledge. Share sales data daily, weekly, monthly.

- Share cost data. See that each person knows what it costs to deliver a service or make a product. Perhaps even give customers cost information. Think what it would be like if a new car dealer gave us honest information about the cost and price of a new car. We would probably be that dealer's customer for life.

- Share profit and loss data for the plant or division. Most employees don't know the economic realities for the division they work in.

Career Development

- Give employees exact information on where they stand and how they are rated. Explain the rating system and salary ranges. If people are given color codes on present performance or potential, tell them what their colors are. Give people this information whether or not they ask for it. A lot of companies will only share such information under pressure. It may open up a short-term hornet's nest, but it is the quickest way out of a patriarchal "I will look out for your best interest, trust me, trust me" relationship.

- Post all jobs. Many companies post the lower-level jobs. Why not include top jobs too?

Possible Changes in Direction, Goals, or Structure

- If we are thinking of changing direction, goals, or even structure, it is important that we talk to people before our plans are firm. Tell people as much as you can, as early as you can. Dialogue takes place before the options are clarified and approval is received. The mind-set is that people who work for us have the maturity and strength to live with the uncertainty about what is going to happen. We want to act as if people care enough about doing the right thing, even if that possibly may not be in their own narrow personal self-interest. The risk in early disclosure is that others may be upset about our plans and mount resistance before we are ready to defend ourselves. What is so bad about that? Our purpose is to serve the business, not just to have our own way. We want our opponents to be as strong as possible and give them all the ammunition we can so as to strengthen ourselves and what we are trying to do.

Participative Restructuring

- As soon as you begin to feel a new structure is needed, tell your people what you are thinking and why. Give people the opportunity to get involved. Who says people cannot be objective about their own jobs—even eliminate them. Little is held so divine as the right of a manager to reorganize a department without having to consult the people being shifted. If a structure isn't working, or if two groups or even two companies are being merged, let the people reorganize themselves. Banks are currently having a feast on each other. They are merging like crazy to stave off the big-city invaders. In one situation, we brought together the managers of two soon-to-be-merged bank operations departments and asked them to decide on the new structure. They were able to do it, putting aside their territorial instincts that normally would have taken years to resolve. If in fact our unit were our own business, we would have no choice but to restructure ourselves. It is painful to have to face the elimination of one's own separate function, but people do it; they survive, and in the process some deeper faith in their potential is reaffirmed.

It is also possible to involve our users in discussions about changes in structure. Our users are affected by internal changes we make; why not let them know about it early so they can have a voice if they choose.

Disclosing Vulnerability

- If a project is not going well and there's some failure, this needs to be part of the public dialogue so people know how to act and how to proceed. To protect a project that is failing by telling people that it's under study and we'll let them know later what the outcome is takes responsibility away from those involved in that project. The alternative is to say that this project is in trouble, we're talking about whether to keep it alive or not, and to be very specific about the nature of the difficulties. Most of the efforts to understand why projects fail indicate that people knew early on that the project couldn't work, but they were afraid that if they delivered the bad news, they would be shot. To keep the harsh realities of our work lives private is to reinforce the notion that to be a messenger of bad news is to commit suicide. Our intent is for people to feel supported for delivering bad news.

The foregoing are just a few areas in which providing "open information" in most organizations can be a political act. The reluctance we have in sharing more information generally runs along two lines: (1) People don't want to hear it. (2) We could lose a competitive advantage.

"People don't want to hear it."   No one likes to hear bad news. But this doesn't mean they cannot handle it. Of course I don't like hearing my boss tell me that not only am I not a star in my unit but that I am languishing somewhere in the middle of the ratings and my future is going to look pretty much like my present. I am not thrilled when mistakes in my group become known to others, and I am not thrilled to find out that my group is one of the ones targeted to be restructured in an effort to cut cost and be more efficient. Despite my discomfort at hearing this information, it is in my best interest to know it. Knowing what is happening gives me choice and treats me like an adult/partner. Withholding discomforting news from people treats them like a volatile or fragile child. It reinforces their dependency. Why should we create policies that adapt to the most dependent people instead of creating policies aimed at the most secure.

The other argument against shielding people from bad news is that it just doesn't work. Whether through the grapevine or plain intuition, people generally know what is going on. We work very hard to decide what to tell and when to tell it, and by the time we get around to communicating, everybody knows. Delaying bad news reduces people's trust in us and their belief that we have trust and confidence in them. Through these small acts of caution, we end up creating the kind of bureaucratic and "political" organization that we wish to change.

"We would lose a competitive advantage."   The other fear in sharing more information about costs, forecasts, plans, quality is that the information will reach our competitors outside the organization and they will use the information against us. Every organization does live in a competitive environment, whether it is a business competing for market share, a hospital competing for patients and doctors, or a volunteer agency

competing for donations or volunteer time. This means there is some information that we want to keep secret. Plans for new products, new territories, new prices fall in this category. The amount of information that "if our competitors knew it, would hurt us" is actually quite narrow. What happens is that attitudes about the "external enemy" invade our internal operation so that competitiveness, caution, and secrecy characterize relationships between groups and people within our own company. External competition is used as the rationale for breeding internal strife. Competition itself is not the problem; most of us love to compete. It is how we go about competing that makes the difference. If internal competitiveness is leading us to withhold information, to be cautious and secretive with each other, we get in trouble. The fact that we are in a competitive industry and that there is some information that cannot be shared is no reason to be cautious and withholding in our dealings with each other.

USE LANGUAGE THAT DESCRIBES REALITY. The third way to develop nonmanipulative strategies is to use language that describes reality rather than masking reality. This idea is very much akin to the preceding ideas about sharing as much information as possible. We not only want to be open about events and plans, but we want to share them in a way that the message gets through. If we are forced to lay off or fire people, we tell them they are being laid off. We don't talk about downsizing, deselecting, restacking, dislodging, or career reevaluation opportunities.

No one likes cutbacks. We all want to be a part of a growing business in which there are more openings than people to fill them. Unfortunately for many organizations, those days are a thing of the past. So if we are cutting by 20 percent, we tell people we are cutting. When possible, we ask people to help us figure out how to cut back. They can often find ways to save costs short of firing people. When possible, we also avoid making flat 20 percent across the board cuts, which just punish the managers who have already brought their costs in line. Basically, we tell people in unmistakable terms where we stand and why we need to take the action we are taking. If we think that we cannot tell people the real reason why we are cutting back because they wouldn't take it well, maybe we should reevaluate that reason.

When we are disappointed in people's actions, we tell them just that. "I am disappointed in you for these reasons." Plain and simple. No more telling others we are giving them negative feedback because we think it will be helpful to them in their future development.

AVOID REPOSITIONING FOR THE SAKE OF ACCEPTANCE. In an effort to build support, we take great pains to justify our project in terms of the popular issue of the moment. We want to look as if we are swimming with the stream. In lean times, everything we do is justified on the basis that it will cut costs and streamline our function. In good times we claim our ideas will help the business grow. A good example of this occurs in the field of management training. In many ways, the focus of training has been quite constant over the last ten to fifteen years. Managers are taught to be goal directed, set clear objectives, be more participative, and in general treat people well. The way that we describe the training, though, changes with the shifting tide. A while ago, essentially the same programs were called *relationship improvement programs*; then they were called *productivity programs*; then they were called *corporate culture programs*—and now they are called *achieving excellence programs*. Next we will all be going to *visionary leadership programs* and perhaps even *positive political skills programs*. It is the distortion of a marketing mentality that leads us to sell our projects on the basis of the popular problem of the moment. It is a commitment to form over substance. Instead of changing the way we do business, we change the way we talk about the way we do business.

Positioning and tying our project to the coattails of what is hot ultimately hurts our credibility and our function. As people begin to find out that what they heard was not what they

got, they feel used. Our cleverness always becomes our undo-
ing. The positive political act is to engage in no fads, even if
doing so would help us sell our project. We tell our customers
exactly what they are getting. We tell top management exactly
what our project is about. No public relations in the rah-rah
sense, no repositioning just for the sake of selling our ideas.
People need to hear both sides of our story. Our certainty and
our doubt.

SUMMARY

The entrepreneurial cycle shown here becomes the underlying
belief system required for an empowered way of operating
(Figure 7). The contract, self-interest, and tactics become the
basis for nurturing autonomy over dependency. It is not possible to overlay positive political actions on top of patriarchy,
self-centeredness, and manipulation. Autonomy with compassion is the essential condition for empowering ourselves
and those around us. Empowerment and positive politics become one and the same.

The key to positive politics, then, is to look at each encounter as an opportunity to support autonomy and to create an
organization of our own choosing. It requires viewing ourselves as the primary instrument for changing the culture.
Cultures get changed in a thousand small ways, not by dramatic announcements emanating from the boardroom. If we
wait until top management gives leadership to the change we
want to see, we miss the point. For us to have any hope that our
own preferred future will come to pass, we provide the leadership. We hope that the world around us supports our vision,
but even if it doesn't, we will still act on that vision. Leadership
is the process of translating intentions into reality. If our
intention is to work in an organization in which authority
resides within the person, contribution is self-interest, and
authenticity is the norm, then all we have to do is make sure our
own actions are aligned with our own intentions. Who

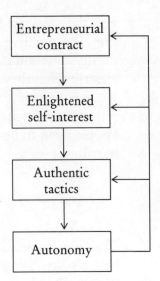

Figure 7.
Entrepreneurial Cycle.

knows—maybe a couple of others will be doing the same, and before long the *Queen Mary* will have changed direction. This is politics at its best, where our actions, not our speeches, become our political statement. Politics as oratory, smoke-filled rooms, back scratching, and bargaining is a game that works but is not worth playing. Learning how to play the game in a way that gives us hope and pride is the purpose of this book.

Part One of this book has focused on the elements of an empowering environment. Part Two focuses on ways we, as managers in the middle, can work on ourselves to become powerful advocates for our unit.

CREATING A VISION OF GREATNESS: THE

FIRST STEP TOWARD EMPOWERMENT

WHERE WE ARE HEADED

It might be helpful at this point to give a chart of where we are headed (Figure 8). This part of the book outlines elements of our own political effectiveness. Empowering ourselves comes from acting on our enlightened self-interest. Politics is the pursuit of self-interest, and positive politics is the pursuit of enlightened self-interest. Step one is to take our enlightened self-interest seriously and give it top priority. Our empowerment is expressed through our personal commitment to each of the elements of enlightened self-interest discussed in Chapter Three.

MEANING, CONTRIBUTION, AND SERVICE.   We need to define what our unit has to offer the organization that will truly make a difference. Meaning comes from the act of creation, and the primary thing we create at work is a successful and useful organization. We decide to build an organization that expresses all of our values about work, achievement, and community. Meaning comes through serving our customers and the people within our unit. Therefore, the first step in implementing an entrepreneurial organization is to create a vision of

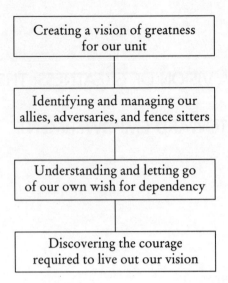

```
┌─────────────────────────────┐
│   Creating a vision of greatness   │
│         for our unit              │
└─────────────────────────────┘
              │
┌─────────────────────────────┐
│   Identifying and managing our    │
│  allies, adversaries, and fence sitters │
└─────────────────────────────┘
              │
┌─────────────────────────────┐
│   Understanding and letting go    │
│   of our own wish for dependency  │
└─────────────────────────────┘
              │
┌─────────────────────────────┐
│   Discovering the courage         │
│   required to live out our vision │
└─────────────────────────────┘
```

Figure 8.
Empowering Ourselves.

greatness for our group. The vision expresses our values and what we hope to contribute.

POSITIVE IMPACT ON OTHERS. We want to build a unit that not only performs tasks well but one that also treats people well. Part of the vision statement deals with how we want people to be treated. We also need to focus on our relationships with those who oppose us. How we deal with our adversaries, and whether we can do so in a way that aligns with our vision, is the test of commitment to creating an authentic and compassionate culture.

INTEGRITY AND MASTERY. Mastery is our commitment to learning, especially about how to use ourselves in a productive way. Integrity is our willingness to live out our vision, even against all odds.

CLAIMING OUR AUTONOMY BY CREATING A VISION

Autonomy is the decision we make to act on our own choice. The most fundamental choice we make is to create a future of our own choosing. In some ways, the future is the cause of our current behavior.[4] We have a vision or an image of where we wish to head and the kind of organization we wish to create, and we act in ways that we believe are in pursuit of creating that future.

The alternative, which is the dependent choice, is to act on a future of someone else's creation. We ask the organization to tell us its vision, its values, and how it wants us to operate, and then that becomes our guidepost.

The payoff for autonomy is that we live our own life and have control over our own destiny. The payoff for dependency is that if we act on someone else's choice and it does not work out well, it is not our fault. Dependency is the wish not to be responsible and held accountable for our actions or our direction. It is the choice for innocence. Autonomy is the choice for guilt. When we act on our own choices, we define our own future. The good news is we have the sense of being in control of our lives. The bad news is that it's our fault and there's no one else to blame.

The initial step toward autonomy for those of us in organizations is to put into words the future we wish to create for our own unit. This is called a vision of greatness. We describe a preferred future that we are committing ourselves to and committing our unit to. The belief is that this vision will be good for the individual, good for the unit, and good for the organization. Creating this vision is our essential act of leadership.

The bureaucratic orientation involves asking people above us, top management, to define the future they wish for the organization. If there is no vision at the top of the organization, we are off the hook. Organizations are so complex and so large, it's often very difficult for a top management group to articulate an understandable vision of the future. Even if top management does create a vision, as many companies are now

---

[4] Thanks to Joel Henning for the concept that our current actions can be understood by looking at the future we desire. It is a hopeful way of looking at behavior because it implies that we need not be controlled by our own history.

doing, it is up to each individual employee, in the context of the organization's mission and purpose, to create his or her own vision of the future.

WHAT IS A VISION AND WHY IS IT IMPORTANT?

Creating a vision forces us to take a stand for a preferred future. It makes the entrepreneurial cycle work because it gives us something we are willing to risk for. The vision is also our way of discovering that serving the organization also serves our self-interest.

We give leadership when we create a vision that positions our unit in relation to the customer and our own colleagues. Our vision channels our deepest values into the workplace and becomes a word picture of how we want our values to be lived out in our unit.

Not just any vision will do. Because we choose to pursue our vision in the marketplace, it needs to be both *strategic* and *lofty*.[5] The strategic element of a vision involves staying focused on our customers/users and expressing in the vision how we contribute to the mission of the organization. This helps connect each activity in our unit with something important, namely, the success of the business.

The vision needs to be lofty in order to capture our imagination and engage our spirit. Inspired performance is characterized by a lofty vision. When the vision for our unit is an expression of our own values, we stay aligned with the organization at a very personal level. Our enlightened self-interest is reinforced when we can commit ourselves to something that matters.

Our vision is our deepest expression of what we want. This declaration of a desired future creates the conditions for having

---

[5] Framing the vision this way is the creation of Bob Anderson. He has been helpful in both making the notion of vision more practical and being a role model for what committing ourselves to living out a vision looks like.

an aligned team. The vision works because only if others know what we want can they support us. It is the dialogue about vision that helps us connect with each other in a way that matters. Our vision can, at times, be a source of conflict, but more often it is a source of connection.

Our vision is very different from our goals and objectives. Goals and objectives are basically a prediction of what is to come. Predictions of what we are going to do in the next week or month or quarter are basically an extension of what we have done the last week or month or quarter. As a result, goals and objectives tend to be rather limited and, in some ways, are rather depressing. Research by Ron Lippitt indicates that during the course of goal-setting meetings, participants become more and more depressed. This discouragement occurs in part because it reinforces the belief that the future will be no different from the past.

An antidote to the feeling that the future will be much like the past is letting go of the objectives and beginning to articulate a vision for our unit. A vision is the preferred future, a desirable state, an ideal state. It is an expression of optimism despite the bureaucratic surrounding or the evidence to the contrary. We dramatize the need for optimism by asking ourselves not only to create a vision but to make it *great*. The word *greatness* is in many ways a very threatening word. When you ask people to create a vision of greatness, they respond by saying, "Can't we create a vision of progress—a vision of excellence—a vision of next steps?"

The wish to hedge against the word *greatness* is to hedge against committing ourselves to something we may not be able to achieve. We fear that greatness is simply not in our story but only in the story of others. Greatness demands that we eliminate caution, that we eliminate our reservations, and that we have hope in the face of the history of our limitations.

The dependent side of ourselves wishes to take a predictable path and to choose maintenance instead of greatness. This is the bureaucratic choice. If we choose to maintain what we now have, we know that is a goal that we can probably accomplish.

The dependent side of ourselves feels that leadership essentially lies with other people. The act of leadership is fundamentally the act of articulating a vision and acting in pursuit of that vision. If we basically believe that the leadership of this organization lies in the hands of others, then we are destined to have a maintenance orientation about our own unit. The belief that leadership lies in the hands of others and the future is for others to decide is our desire to stay away from the frontier. The frontier represents danger, unpredictability, and essential loss of control. Better to stay on the East Coast, with developed cities, modern conveniences, and predictable environment, even if it's not to our satisfaction, than to head West with the wagon trains into uncharted territory and certain danger.

To take the safe path in an organization is to avoid the frontier and to ask others to chart that territory for us. In our dependency, we surround ourselves with corporate insulation. We demand a lot of data before we make a decision; we act in the short run because it's more predictable and under our control. We only do those things that have extremely visible results because we can measure progress and defend ourselves against accusations that what we're doing is not working.

When we choose the frontier, we're choosing an unmeasurable and unknowable future. This is a vulnerable choice because if we are forced to explain why we choose that future, how we're going to get there, or whether that future is possible, we have no solid response that we can count on. Moving toward the frontier, creating a vision of greatness, demands an act of faith. Faith, by its nature, is unmeasurable and indefensible through the use of data and external evidence. An act of faith moving toward a preferred future is a leap beyond what is now being experienced. This act of faith and act of courage are demanded of each of us if we wish to choose autonomy and put our survival into our own hands.

Faith in our ability to find meaning and be of service is expressed by our vision. Putting into words our own vision of greatness for the future has several effects on us.

1. In an implicit way, it signifies our disappointment with what exists now. To articulate our vision of the future is to come out of the closet with our doubts about the organization and the way it operates, our doubts about the way our unit serves its customers, and our doubts about the way we deal with each other inside the organization.

2. The vision exposes the future that we wish for our unit and opens us up to potential conflict with the visions of other people. We know in our hearts that visions are not negotiable, and therefore we run the risk of conflicting visions when we put them into words with each other.

3. Articulating a vision of greatness also forces us to hold ourselves accountable for acting in a way that is congruent with that vision. The vision states how we want to work with customers and users, and the vision states how we want to work with each other. Once we have created a vision and communicated it to the people around us, it becomes a benchmark for evaluating all of our actions. This is an uneasy reality to live within. The power of the vision is in the way it forces internal accountability for our actions. If we are acting on someone else's vision, we can justify actions we don't believe in by claiming that we had no choice; they were demanded by the direction that someone else created. You hear this excuse all the time. If we are driven by a vision of our own creation, this excuse disappears and we can no longer make the claim that it's not our fault. We have to listen to the disquieting words of others about how we are not acting in the pursuit of that vision.

The hardest thing for any of us is to live by the rules that we create. It's difficult enough to live by the rules that others create. It is brutal and fierce to live by the rules that we create. When we create the vision for our unit, we create a set of requirements and demands on ourself, simply because they're our own creation.

To avoid creating a vision for oneself is to protect oneself from disappointment and failure. It is hard to comprehend how pervasive this wish for protection is. When we ask people to change, the first conversation is about the risks of changing. When we do training in workshops and try to give people new skills, their first question is "Does top management support these new skills and behaviors?" A tremendous amount of literature and thinking says that every change program has to start at the top and has to be fully supported by top management before one can expect people in the middle and at the bottom to move in any direction. This belief in "top down" change is a wish to be protected.

To choose autonomy and create our own vision is to choose a risky path. It is to act on the belief that there is no safe path. Any future we move toward has hazards, and the fact that what we do has risks is a sign that we're headed in the right direction. When we choose protection and opt to maintain what we already have, we believe that what we have accomplished is enough. It's a willingness to stand on our laurels.

The choice for maintenance expresses the desire to get out of the stock market and put our money in a safe place, knowing that there is enough there for us to wade into shore. When we ask people to move in the direction of their own autonomy, we ask them to bet their savings. This violates the patriarchal contract most of us have with large organizations. We join large organizations because we think we'll be safe and "they" will provide for our future. Unfortunately, we may discover too late that the "safe" path was not very safe.

The first step in choosing autonomy, then, is to create our own vision of greatness for our function. When we create a vision of greatness, we give meaning to what we are doing, knowing all along that the odds of achieving greatness are small. Greatness is the entrepreneurial choice. It is the belief, whether we like it or not, that leadership is solely up to us. It is the choice to live on the frontier, to avoid insulation, and to choose the cold, knowing that we may in some way fail and be disappointed. The mere fact that we call it a vision raises the question of whether it's really achievable, and in fact visions may not be and often are not achievable.

Positive political skills and the entrepreneurial path are initiated by our statement of the desired future. Our actions are then totally in pursuit of that vision. To create the vision and act in pursuit of it is to be autonomous, entrepreneurial, and political in a positive sense. Doing this is political because it goes against the norms that dominate most large or middle-sized organizations. Most organizations, for the reasons described in Part One, emphasize safety, control, and dependency. Thus, to choose autonomy and to create our own vision is to move against the tide. Any act against the tide in pursuit of a vision or a purpose is a political act. It is an act in our own self-interest; it is an act that advocates something we believe in, and by its nature it is political.

WHAT IF WE DON'T HAVE A VISION? A vision statement is an expression of optimism. Often when you ask individuals what their vision of greatness is, they say they don't have a vision of greatness. The response to that is to say, "Suppose you had a vision of greatness; what would it be?" A vision exists within each of us, even if we have not made it explicit or put it into words. Our reluctance to articulate our vision is a measure of our despair and a reluctance to take responsibility for our own lives, our own unit, and our own organization. A vision statement is an expression of hope, and if we have no hope, it is hard to create a vision.

THE DIFFERENCE BETWEEN A VISION AND A MISSION STATEMENT. A vision is really a dream created in our waking hours of how we would like the organization to be. It differs from a mission statement in that a mission statement is a statement of what business we are in and sometimes our ranking in that business.

The mission statement names the game we are going to play. As an example, a large health care company's mission statement is "to market health care products that have a demonstrable health benefit to the customer, to be the leader in each product line, to return a fair profit to our stockholders, and to provide good opportunities to our employees." This

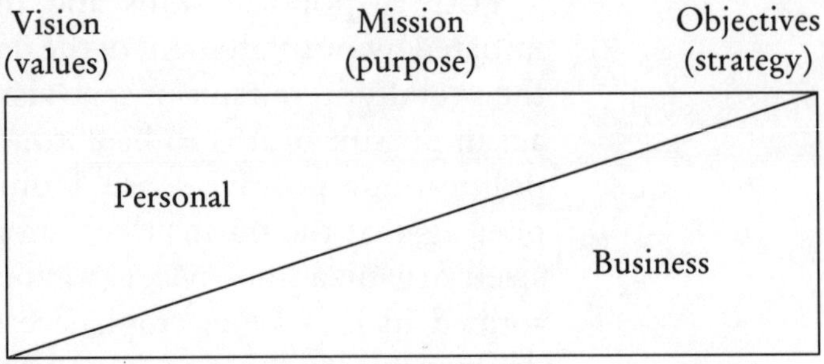

Figure 9.
Vision, Mission, and
Objectives.

| Vision
(values) | Mission
(purpose) | Objectives
(strategy) |

Personal

Business

tells us something about the business the company is choosing. "Demonstrable health benefit" means no cosmetics or other personal care products. "Leader in each product line" means if the company can't grab a major market share it isn't going to try. "Fair profit" means certain margins and return on investment are required. This is more business focused than a vision. A vision is more a philosophy about how we are going to manage the business. Figure 9 contrasts vision, mission, and objectives.

There is nothing new or unique about creating a vision statement. Many organizations have had a vision for many years. They may call it something different, such as a credo, set of core values, or guiding principles. In the last three years almost every company has developed a statement of values in its effort to articulate what its culture is. What is unique is the orientation that it is the task of each employee, not just top management, to create a vision of greatness. The common pattern is for top management to spend six months defining a vision and then to put great emphasis on communicating it downward throughout the organization. The belief is that the act of leadership is to create a vision and then to enroll the rest of the organization in supporting that vision. One executive said, only half joking, "Let's rent Candlestick Park [a sports stadium outside San Francisco] and have all 43,000 of our employees marching in support of our vision." A rewarding fantasy for the executive, but a dependency-creating process for the employees. The act of creating and communicating a vision is an act of leadership, and each employee needs to do this. The process begins at the top, but the additional step that is required is then to demand that each level beneath the top group do the same. It is the job of each manager to create a vision for the unit. The vision of top management and the people above becomes input for the vision created by each lower level manager and employee. All individuals who want to be entrepreneurial and to take ownership for the business have to create their own vision.

Since most people beneath the top have not struggled with creating their own vision, what follows are some guidelines for doing just that. The guidelines cover three basic steps: creating the vision, communicating our vision, and coaching others in creating their vision. For simplicity's sake the guidelines for the first step will be stated in the form of tips.

CREATING THE VISION

Here are some thoughts on how to begin to create your vision.

TIP NO. 1: FORGET ABOUT BEING NUMBER ONE.   You can't watch television these days without having someone stick an index finger in your face and shout, "We're number one, we're number one!" The wish to be on top, the desire for recognition, fame, fortune, profits, the bottom line, all reflect a myopic self-interest to get ahead. They don't belong in our vision statement. The vision statement expresses the contribution we want to make to the organization, not what the external world is going to bestow upon us. The choice for greatness is an act of service and an expression of our enlightened self-interest. If there is justice in the world, we will be rewarded for our good work. We claim our independence by focusing on the good work, not on where we end up in the standings. The vision of greatness is a statement of what we offer our customers and each other, and we commit to the vision because the vision is worth pursuing for its own sake. If we get rewarded for making the vision happen, we will accept the recognition gracefully—but that is not why we pursue it.

TIP NO. 2: DON'T BE PRACTICAL.   We live in a pragmatic culture in which we have been taught to set specific measurable objectives and to have a work plan or a chart on our wall that shows how we are going to meet those objectives. Our desire to be practical works against the creation of a vision. A vision of greatness expresses the spiritual and idealistic side of our nature. It is a preferred future that comes from the heart, not from the head. Being practical too quickly acts as a restraint on the vision. Our purpose in creating the vision is to clarify the kind of unit we wish to create, knowing all along that we may never get there. The vision is a lighthouse giving us direction rather than a specific destination. The last thing we want to ask someone who is creating a vision is "How are you going to get there?"

TIP NO. 3: BEGIN WITH YOUR CUSTOMERS.   The long-term survival of an organization is dependent upon how well the organization stays in touch with and serves its internal and external customers. In the short run it can sustain itself through price increases, cost control, or a friendly banker, but ultimately the reality of the marketplace determines the organization's future. This also applies to a department operating within a larger organization.

The mind-set required to be an entrepreneur for our unit is to view other units within the company as either our customers or our suppliers. The group next in line receiving our product or service is a customer of ours. Viewing this group as a customer acts as a restraint on complaints about how it uses what we give it. Most of the fights and conflict in organizations occur between units and people at the same level. The rules are fairly clear about how we work with bosses and subordinates, but they are very unclear about how we work with those at the same level. We don't know how much power and control we have over our equals. In fact, sometimes we don't know whether we should be competing with them or collaborating with them.

The way through this competitive/collaborative ambivalence is for each function to ask itself who its internal customers/users are and to create a vision, a preferred future, of how it wants to work with them. Then we are ready to ask some additional useful questions:

1. If our internal customers/users were the only customers we had, how would we treat them?

2. How can we use their frustration and disappointment with us as a learning experience to teach us how to improve our way of doing business? We learn how to serve our marketplace mostly through dissatisfied customers. To learn from dissatisfied customers, we have to move toward them, treat them with respect, and listen to them very carefully, without being defensive.

3. How do we deliver bad news to our users? Sometimes we cannot fulfill our promises to them. How early do we tell them? When we let them down, do we blame it on someone else or take responsibility for our mistakes?

4. How do we handle situations in which our customers let us down? What do we do when they are inaccurate in defining their needs, when they owe us information and we either don't get it or get it so late that it undermines our schedules? We have the choice of whether to use this as an excuse, blame the customers, or have the orientation that we should help our customers become better at their own business. It is part of our function to help customers be more effective in their own way of operating. We are consultants to our customers, constantly showing them ways to better work with us.

Here are some examples of ideas from a variety of vision statements about what greatness looks like when we are dealing with customers:

- We act as partners with our customers.

- We are committed to our customers' success, and we encourage them to teach us how to do business with them.

- Our customers leave us feeling understood.

- The purpose of a sales call is to help the customer make a good decision.

- We fulfill every promise, meet every requirement.

- We have the courage to say no.

- We choose quality over speed.

- We don't cover up bad news.

- We don't want customers who care only about cost. They will pay a premium for quality service, being understood, and our commitment to their success.

- We want everyone involved to express real feelings and stay engaged.

- We want to understand the impact of our actions on our customers.

- We offer and expect forgiveness from our customers.

- Our customers are as important as our shareholders.

- We exceed their expectations.

- We don't force solutions on our customers.

- We are here to help, not to police.

- Our dissatisfied customers teach us how to sell to those who currently do not use our service or product.

All of these statements make sense. It is up to us to decide which ones are personally important to us and what similar additional statements we want to make for our own unit. The power of these statements is that they become the internally generated rules by which we hold ourselves accountable. If you want to take a taste of the meal instead of just continuing to read the menu, take a minute right now and write down some statements of your vision of greatness in working with your customers.

TIP NO. 4: YOU CAN'T TREAT YOUR CUSTOMERS ANY BETTER THAN YOU TREAT EACH OTHER.   An additional vital element in a vision is how we treat each other within the unit. Each of our customers wants a unique and understanding response from us. If, within the unit, we are cautious, competitive, and judgmental with each other, we won't be able to give our customers the response they want. Sales people in a store treat us much the same as they are being treated. If we, as customers, are being ignored, they as employees are probably being ignored. If they are cold, indifferent, and unresponsive, we have some very good clues as to the management style of their supervisors. We have to manage our own people in a way that is absolutely aligned with the way we want our customers and users to be managed. We can't use fear and punishment to improve customer service. Our employees' ultimate revenge is to take out on our customers resentment and frustration that should rightfully be aimed at us.

Our own unit is also our testing ground for discovering what is possible for organizations. One of our primary purposes is to create within our own unit a model of how we want the whole organization to function. Here are some useful questions for creating a vision for the internal operation of your unit:

1. How do you want support to be expressed within the group? In most groups support is expressed by leaving people alone. As long as you do not make a mistake, I won't bother you. The alternative is to believe that people need to learn what they are doing right.

Appreciation can be expressed directly, credit given freely, celebrations held for successes.

2. How do you want conflict and disagreement managed? Traditional methods are to avoid, smooth over, or arm wrestle under pressure. People go to an umpire when they get stuck. You may decide you want to value compassionate confronting or negotiating behavior as vital to the unit.

3. What is the balance you want between having a team operation and having a series of competent individuals with clearly separated areas of responsibility? Many groups talk about teamwork but really operate on a one-to-one basis with their boss.

4. Competition within departments or between departments is a mixed motive situation. We know we are supposed to work together, yet almost all of the performance evaluation systems have people competing with each other. What stance do you want to take on internal competition? The president of a West Coast garment manufacturer decided he was going to evaluate his key executives according to how much they contributed to each other's success. Radical idea.

An endless number of values can get expressed in stating how we want people to work together. It is up to all of us to ask ourselves which are the values and beliefs we hold most dearly about human interaction. These very personal values drive our vision of greatness for the people within our group. Here are some more examples of statements people have made:

- We want consistency between our plans and actions.

- A willingness to share.

- Disagree without fear.

- Commitment to a long-term strategy.

- Create a safe workplace.

- We want to live our values.

- Have each person connected with the final product.

- Treat each person in a unique way.

- Overcome levels and hierarchy.

- Our employees are as important as our stockholders.

- Our people are the business.

- A positive attitude, less energy on bad situations.

- We want to see caring and love in all our actions.

- Every person is responsible for building the business.

- Work as a team.

- Each person has a place at the table.

- Each person feels valued and respected.

- Provide meaningful work.

- Managers exist to serve their employees.

- Eliminate nonproductive work.

- Each person has the right to say no.

- Control of our own destiny.

- Freedom to fail. People are shot only for not trying.

- Honesty at all times.

- Empathy for others' pain.

- Each person is heard and understood.

As with the vision statements about our customers, these statements are compelling. It is up to us to know our own values and decide which we want expressed through our work. Take another minute here and think about your own vision of greatness for the people you work with.

TIP NO. 5: IF YOUR VISION STATEMENT SOUNDS LIKE MOTHERHOOD AND APPLE PIE AND IS SOMEWHAT EMBARRASSING, YOU ARE ON THE RIGHT TRACK. A vision is an expression of hope and idealism. It oversimplifies the world and implies that anything is possible. The embarrassment we may feel is really our vulnerability at taking a stance of innocence in the midst of an environment that seems sophisticated, hard-nosed, and pragmatic. Surrounded by a preoccupation with safety, control, and approval, we stand naked and declare that there are certain deeper values, often spiritual ones, that we are giving top priority. We bet the farm on a set of values about customers and our own people and pray that the world will support us. Others tell us it is a jungle out there, and we say, "No it's not; that's only foliage." The vulnerability we feel means we are moving against the culture or working to recreate the culture, and that is what makes a strong vision statement a positive political act. At the very moment we are identifying and communicating our vision, we are living the kind of organization we have wished all along to create.

We know we create a great vision when it has three qualities:

1. *It comes from the heart.* A vision is in some ways unreasonable. The heart knows no reason. When our vision asks too much of us, we should begin to trust it.

2. *We, alone, can make this statement.* The statement needs to be recognizable as ours. It needs to be personal, and those who know us should be able to recognize who it came from.

3. *It is radical and compelling.* A vision dramatizes our wishes. This makes it radical and demanding. Radical in the best sense of service rather

than rejection. Our willingness to take a unique stand is what empowers us.

SOME EXAMPLES OF THE CHOICE FOR GREATNESS. People at the top of organizations are now creating a vision for their company. Examples of a few of these visions follow. What is even more encouraging is that individual managers are committing themselves to a vision for their department. Some of the examples are very short, some a little wordy; all are compelling.

Electrical and Electronics Division, Ford Motor Company

- Have a directed destiny.

- The customer is king.

- People are our most important resources.

- Treat suppliers as we wish to be treated.

- Become the standard by which others are judged.

The Greenwich Workshop (Fine Art Dealer)

- The collector comes first.

- Quality is reputation.

- Art demands originality.

Cliff Bolster, Vice-President of Human Resources, Bath Iron Works

- Treat every person with whom we come in contact with respect and dignity.

- Deal with the divisions we service as if they are valued customers and, if they chose to, could find another source for the services we provide.

- Demonstrate by our actions, the way we want the whole company to operate.

- Minimize discussing and writing and maximize acting and doing to achieve our objectives.

- Take full responsibility for the quality of our departments' performance and don't blame others.

- Never hear the phrase "That's not my job."

- Give each other feedback on what we want from each other.

- Recognize achievement and celebrate success.

The next vision statement was written by Bob Haas, president and chief executive officer of Levi Strauss and Company. What is so impressive about it is that it affirms a set of values with the belief that these are the values that will best serve the bottom line and the customer. What is also impressive is the commitment made by a group of top executives that their primary job is to be the ones who personally act on these values in their dealings with each other and the rest of the organization.

GREATNESS FOR LS&CO.

I want LS&Co. to become and to be known as a great company. Our greatness will reflect a commitment to excellence in everything we do and with all constituents. We will achieve greatness through a commitment to the following goals and practices:

People
- Establish a climate of openness, mutual respect and teamwork.

- Encourage initiative and risk-taking.

- Create a small-company environment.

- Value each employee as an individual; profit from diversity.

- Maximize personal contributions, sense of involvement.

- Maximize individual development and sense of fulfillment.

- Minimize policies; emphasize individual responsibility; achieve full understanding of company values and direction. This becomes the basis for individual commitment and action.

- Recognize contribution and excellence.

- Ensure that everyone understands how he/she can contribute and where he/she stands.

- Provide a safe, wholesome working environment that is stimulating, pleasant and supports maximum personal effectiveness.

- Create a caring, "family" environment.

- Link company and employee interests.

- Commitment to "ego-less" management; the welfare of the company and its people transcends individual goals and concerns.

- Support maximum individual productivity.

- Emphasize compassion and flexibility so that human needs (rather than rules and policies) are met.

Customers

- Ensure that LS&Co. products are *demonstrably superior* and provide the highest performance (appearance, durability, comfort, style) and at the fairest price (value).

- Make product innovation a hallmark of LS&Co.

- Handle customer inquiries, concerns and complaints in a prompt, fair and courteous manner.

- Advertise and promote LS&Co. products in a truthful, respectful and engaging manner in association with wholesome non-exploitive media and programming.

Accounts (Retail Stores)

- Assist each account in achieving maximum profitability and desired market position with our merchandise.

- Provide superior service.

- Be viewed as knowledgeable of each account's needs and a helpful source of support and business counsel.

- Be valued for superior account relations (courtesy, integrity, responsiveness).

Suppliers

- Encourage long-standing, mutually profitable business relationships.

- Develop the highest component quality standards (fabric, sundries, etc.); clearly define expectations and assist suppliers in achieving satisfactory performance.

- Involve suppliers in solving problems and developing innovative and superior products.

- Be viewed as knowledgeable of each supplier's capabilities and needs and a helpful source of support and business counsel.

- Be valued for superior supplier relations (courtesy, integrity, responsiveness).

The final vision statement is from my own small consulting company. It is a little embarrassing to put this in here, and it sounds a little like motherhood and apple pie, but since this whole section is about creating a vision, I seem to have no choice but to include it.

Designed Learning

1. We treat all people who come in contact with us as members of our organization. Each client, supplier, and member of the larger community that contacts us feels understood and cared for. They experience us as acting with integrity even when we choose not to give them what they want. They have the feeling that we are in business to serve and not to exploit others for financial gain. We treat all as family members, and we want each to experience something of value as a result of the contact with us.

2. We are committed to providing the highest quality, people, learning designs, and materials that are within our capability. Quality means we are congruent with our deepest human values, we deal with underlying issues in our clients, not just the surface ones, and our services are practical and immediately usable. We are in the education business and believe quality education confronts the whole person, tells the truth, and aims right at the center of an issue. Quality means that we will not provide services where they are not needed, even if on occasion a client would be willing to hire us inappropriately. We take our commitments very seriously and we only promise what we can deliver.

3. We market by giving clients as much as we have every moment we are with them. We don't want to tease, lure, or

create unneeded dependency for the sake of generating more business.

4. We treat our employees and suppliers as well as we treat our clients. Our economic philosophy is to pay our employees as much as we can and charge our clients as little as we can. We want our employees to feel that this is their business and when the business does well they will do well. We also want people to share in the downside risk. If some individuals are not valued highly, they need to know that so that they can make a good decision about their future.

These examples are here simply to give an idea of the kind of focus a vision statement might have. The heart of a vision is not so much in the actual words but in the act of creating it and committing ourself to it. When we create and communicate a vision, we are inviting others to let us know when we are fulfilling it and when we are falling short. That creates accountability for us and is the way we force ourselves to take responsibility for our unit. That's why it is not enough for just top management to create a vision. Every employee needs to go through the process. Once we have a vision, the next steps are to communicate it and to coach others in creating their own vision.

COMMUNICATING OUR VISION

The essence of political skill is building support for our function and our projects. This takes place through dialogue, and the most compelling dialogue we can have is about our vision. Leadership is keeping others focused on the vision, and this means that we have to get comfortable talking about it. We can talk about the vision statement in ways that help command others' interest.

OPTIMISM. We need to communicate hope and optimism. Even though we have doubts about how to reach the vision, it is a statement of a preferred future. If we have committed ourselves to reaching for that future, talking about it with conviction will always be persuasive. Others will often support us simply because of how much we care. The more we talk about the vision, the more committed we become. Our doubts about whether others will support our vision are really a projection of our own doubts. Talking about the vision frequently has the effect of reducing those doubts and allowing us to be more optimistic.

EMOTIONAL CHARGE. We need to feel free to use color and excitement in our language. Words like greatness, service, meaning, perfection, compassion, integrity, love are emotionally charged words that we can get excited about. They may seem out of place in a work environment. They are not literally "out of place"; they are just rare. Emotionally charged words may not belong in a goal-setting conversation, but they are the stuff that visions are made of. Perhaps our unique contribution to our unit is to keep us focused on a deeper set of values than simply costs and productivity. We have to believe that most people are searching for meaning, compassion, and integrity at work and that if we are willing to talk about those things, awkward as it may be, it increases our possibility of finding them.

METAPHORS. Using metaphors, parables, picture images is also helpful. We need an image that has meaning for us, an image that gives others a picture of our vision. People have likened their vision to a variety of things:

- a tree, with a trunk, branches, leaves, seasons, changes, growth;

- the human body, with its different systems, kept going by fresh air and a supply of fresh blood;

- sports teams (a particular favorite of men);

- machinery, cars, airplanes, gyroscopes, radar, submarines;

- a painting, a poem, a string quartet or orchestra.

Which image doesn't matter — only that it is something that we care about.

SPECIFIC PICTURE OF THE FUTURE. The more we can see what the future would look like, the easier it is for us to understand and communicate it to others. It helps sometimes to fantasize that we are in a time capsule, visiting our unit three years from now, and hovering above like a helicopter. Describe what we would see happening. How would we be working with customers and each other? What would meetings look like, what would the budget look like, what would be the nature of our projects, how would people be spending their time, what would the product or service look like as it came out the door?

All of these qualities of a vision statement help us to communicate. Talking about our vision in a vivid way also encourages other people to do the same.

COACHING OTHERS IN CREATING THEIR VISION

An important part of our leadership role is to work with subordinates to help them put into words their own vision of greatness for the future. Our goal is not simply to have others embody *our* vision but to support others in embodying their vision. It is an expression of our belief that there is more than one answer. Often when we ask people what their vision is, they say that they don't have a vision. Don't you believe it. Each of us has hopes for a preferred future; it is just that we get so used to responding to others' expectations of us that our own vision remains at an unconscious level. Saying that we don't have a vision can also be an expression of our pessimism. If the prospect of having any control over our own destiny seems like a remote possibility, it is hard to generate any energy for talking about a future of our own choosing. Don't be seduced by passivity or pessimism. Here is a series of questions we have been using to help people discover their own vision.

1. Pick an important project you are working on that you care about and are frustrated with. Describe the goals of the project and why you are frustrated.

2. Next ask why you care so much about the project. Our frustration is an expression of our commitment. If we were not so committed to a project, we would not be so frustrated. We ask people why they care so much about the project as a way of getting at their deeper values about their work. We all have strong values about doing work that has meaning, being of real service to our customers, treating other people well, and maintaining some integrity in the way we work. Keep asking why, why, why until you hear some statements that seem to come from the heart.

3. Ask what your ideal way of working with your customers looks like. If you revisited your unit three years from now and greatness had been achieved, what would you see happening with customers?

4. Now ask the same questions about the future focusing on how you think people should treat each other in the unit. What personal and even spiritual values would you like to see expressed in the way the group operates internally?

These questions will help begin the dialogue about vision. In coaching others there are three qualities we want to look for in their statements: depth, clarity, and responsibility.

Depth. Since the vision statement comes from the heart, it should be as personal as possible.

Clarity. We can help people to be specific by continually

asking what they would see if greatness became a reality. Vagueness is a way of not making a commitment to the vision.

Responsibility. A major obstacle to creating a vision is a feeling of helplessness. Victims generate boring vision statements. Asking people to create a vision statement is a way of confronting their feeling of helplessness. The primary reason we demand that people create a vision statement is to reinforce the belief that all of us are engaged in the process of creating this organization, whether we admit it or not. We keep urging people to talk about the unit as if it were theirs to transform in any way that they choose.

The coaching process takes patience. After people are first asked to create a vision, it often takes days or weeks before they are able to come up with a statement that they can get excited about. The patience and effort are worth it. The struggle to create a vision is the struggle with hope and whether our unit is in fact ours to create. As managers we begin to empower those around us when we help and gently pressure them to do the same. The vision statement itself becomes an expression of our enlightened self-interest — namely, how our unit provides meaning, service, contribution, integrity, compassion, and mastery. The process of creating the vision serves to reinforce our intention for an entrepreneurial contract. Once we become clear about our vision of greatness, our task is to begin to act on the vision by creating structures, policies, and practices that support it. Actions grow from each of our specific visions and will be idiosyncratic to our own situation.

To add to the menu of possibilities, here are some specific steps several companies are taking to support their vision of creating an entrepreneurial and empowered culture (which is also the vision behind this book). The goal is to have every aspect of organizational life be congruent with the vision. This takes us from policies and practices all the way to office location and decor. Listed below are brief statements of vision and some actions being taken to support those visions.

Vision: Serve the customer above all else.

Action: 1. *Adopt a philosophy that good selling is helping the customer/user make a good decision.*   Our philosophy of selling is to help the buyer make a good decision. This is different from the belief that the purpose of our selling effort is to convince someone to support our project. If we think of top management or of other departments as our customers, our goal is to maintain a high-quality, long-term relationship. We want customers for life. If we convince them to buy something that is not in their best interest, in the short run we get support for our projects; in the long run we have sacrificed our credibility. If through the use of successful persuasive techniques we gain support for a project that does not work or is not really needed, we have, in effect, mortgaged our future.

The pressure is immense in each of us to generate budget support, increase sales, engage in innovative work, and contribute something of unique value to the organization. If we allow that pressure to lead us into making promises we can't keep, we are in trouble. Helping our users make good decisions is a different goal than that of increasing sales, budget, and manpower. A commitment to the quality of our customers' decisions is a positive political act in the midst of a culture that values quantity, size, and growth above all else.

Traditional selling techniques emphasize overcoming objections and closing the deal. The best sales organizations don't worry too much about closing techniques but focus on helping the customer, inside the company or outside the company, feel understood and supported. People buy where they feel understood. Better to help our users make a good decision, even if it means that we don't make the sale, than to sell something that is unneeded or may not work.

2. *Customer contact.*   Everyone, in every department, is given the opportunity to spend time with customers. The concept is that everyone is responsible for customer knowledge.

Vision: Operate as a team in which everyone feels responsible for the success of the team.

Action: 1. *Performance criteria.*   Evaluate subordinates according to what they have done to contribute to the success of their peers. Some managers believe that encouraging competition within the organization acts as a toughening motivational device. Sales people are publicly ranked according to sales performance. Different departments are given the same task to see who can come up with the best or quickest solution. Some individuals get publicly compared to others as a form of praise or motivation. These strategies serve to reinforce the belief that employees are here to advance their own career first and serve the organization second. They have it backwards.

2. *Peer recruitment.*   Teams interview new employees so that each person shares the responsibility for selecting co-workers. Any one team member, including the boss, has veto power over a candidate.

Vision: The physical space reflects the fact that we are all partners in the business and we want to minimize distance and fears between levels in the organization and between different functions.

Action: 1. *Office location.*   Relationships across departments are the difficult ones to manage. Place people from different departments next to each other. As you go down the hall, the sequence of offices might be marketing, finance, government regulation, research and development, manufacturing, and personnel — and then start all over again with a marketing office. A physical reminder that employees are all part of the same organization.

2. *Office size and decor.*   All offices at every level are the same size and of the same attractiveness — comfortable but neither monastic nor luxurious.

3. *Dining rooms.*   Luxury dining rooms and the cafeteria are open to everyone. Top management eats in the cafeteria as an antidote to isolation.

4. *Parking spaces.*   First come, first served. Reward for getting there early.

5. *Meeting rooms.* The physical setting carries a symbolic statement of our intentions of how we want people to communicate with each other. If our intent is that everybody has a piece of the action, then a circle is the form we should choose. When we meet in a circle, there is no head or foot of the table and each person can easily see every other person. Long narrow rooms and tables, which are typical boardroom and executive level arrangements, have the effect of reinforcing power differences. Narrow tables or even U-shaped tables inhibit dialogue because you literally cannot see those sitting on the same side of the table. You have to lean way forward or backward just to make eye contact.

For large management/employee meetings, stay away from the auditorium and use the cafeteria. Auditoriums, with unmovable seats and stages, are designed for a star system. The purpose of employee meetings is to reduce the distance between levels. Let the setting reflect that.

The cafeteria belongs to the employees. Meeting there is a way of management's coming to them. Cafeterias also lack the rigidity of an auditorium. Tables and chairs are movable, there is no stage, and there are no stars.

6. *Get the executives off the top floor.* If top management exists to support and serve the rest of the organization, put executives on the bottom floor. Let them be accessible. The intent is to reduce isolation. Executives don't need status symbols to be motivated and find meaning in their work. Creating physical symbols of status and power simply reinforces the message that we work to pursue our own myopic self-interest. Take away some of the trappings, and we should find out which executives are here to build a business and which are here to look good. We sometimes hear that elegant executive decor is really there to impress outsiders, customers, suppliers, bankers, and the community. This is a fragile rationale. If you really need this, have a few special rooms for this.

Of course we can get carried away with giving the physical setting too much importance. Sometimes a room is just a room. Architects and space planners, however, tend to have a rather traditional, patriarchal view of organization norms, status, and culture. The architecture and decor need to flow from our vision rather than dictate it.

Vision: People should feel support.

Actions: *1. Blame-free meetings.* Create a ground rule forbidding any blaming statements. Be especially strict about blaming anyone not in the room. When we blame absent parties, what we don't realize is at the very instant we are blaming them, they are having the same conversation about us. If people in the room are so frustrated with each other that they have to express their negative feelings before they can get on with the business at hand, then allow twenty minutes of blaming statements. The ground rule for this discussion is that people in the room can *only* make blaming statements and may not defend themselves. After the twenty-minute period of blame is over, take a five-minute break and then reconvene and get on with the agenda.

    2. Give positive feedback. Most organizations are a wasteland of support. It is hard for us to know what we are doing right. Even when we get good results, we aren't sure which of the myriad things we tried made the difference. Specific, positive, personal feedback has a potential that is virtually untapped in most cultures.

    3. Reduce threat as a strategy. The fear of failure has been internalized enough by most people, the organization need do nothing to reinforce fear as a motivational device. Threats and even consistent negative feedback increase caution and indirect strategies. There is already enough in work life to put us on shaky ground without management's using fear as a tool. Most of us are already certain that our sins will be punished and our good deeds go unnoticed.

BUILDING SUPPORT FOR YOUR VISION:

NEGOTIATING WITH ALLIES

AND ADVERSARIES

We now come to the most traditional aspect of political skills coalition and support building.

We may have in mind the actions we would like to take, but we need the support of other people to realize our vision, and they need us. Our wish is that our users, our suppliers, our subordinates, and our bosses will all be aligned with our vision. This chapter explores how to deal with our interdependence and the fact that life is never so simple.

Having created the vision our task is to walk the tightrope between being strong advocates for our beliefs and not terminally alienating others in the process. We want to be empowered but not at others' expense. We do this by choosing to live the entrepreneurial cycle. This means we contract with ourselves to accomplish the following:

1. Support the authority that comes from within ourselves. Our vision statement begins this.

2. Express ourselves. We let others know how we feel, what we want, and where we stand.

3. Commit ourselves to acting out in our unit how we want the whole organization to operate.

The difficult part is to move toward the vision in a way that affirms our commitment to be of service, to contribute, and to treat others with compassion. In other words—our enlightened self-interest. We want to win, but not by any means. Remember Allan, whose vision of creating an entrepreneurial division was both strategic and lofty; his aggressive and at times disdainful way of dealing with those above him ultimately led to his downfall.

What is critical is both to have the vision and to negotiate our projects in a positive way. Being right is not enough. We approach each encounter knowing that the way we deal with our adversaries and allies is how we foster an organization of our own choosing.

THE CRITICAL SKILLS: NEGOTIATING AGREEMENT AND NEGOTIATING TRUST

Those whom we need to influence become our adversaries and allies on the basis of two dimensions: agreement and trust. We either agree or disagree about where we are headed, and we either trust or distrust each other about the way we operate in pursuit of that future. Agreement or conflict can take place over the rather abstract statement of our vision or, more frequently, over project purpose, goals, and requirements. Trust is almost universally built or destroyed on the basis of issues of justice and integrity.

Using these two dimensions of agreement and trust, we can create a matrix on which to place those people in our constellation.

Step one in developing a political strategy is to identify who among our customers, bosses, subordinates, and bystanders we need for the success of our project. Each of these people can then be placed somewhere on the matrix. Depending on our level of agreement and the level of trust, we can develop an approach for each person. The approach for most encounters is to work through three steps:

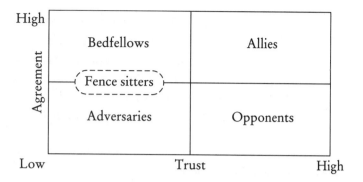

1. Exchange vision, purpose, or goals.

2. Affirm or negotiate agreement.

3. Affirm or negotiate trust.

What follows is an exploration of each box of the matrix. The trick is to figure out where our stakeholders stand and then to influence them in a way that aligns with our vision and self-interest.

We become political at the moment we attempt to translate our vision into action. The first question then is "Who shares our intentions and our vision?" We discover our support through the dialogue we have with the people around us. The enrollment process begins with finding out whether others around us share our vision or at least have a vision of the future that is compatible with ours. It is rare that other people's visions will be identical to our own, but it is very common that our vision and the visions of other people can comfortably coexist.

We discover who shares our vision by getting in the habit of talking about it. I tell you what I am trying to create, and I ask you what future you are committed to. It is easy to make assumptions about others' positions without actually asking them. Sometimes we think people are adversaries simply from either their reputations or what we infer from a distance. Don't ever believe that someone is an adversary simply because of what friends may say about the person. Hearsay information is inadmissible in court, and it should be inadmissible in our deciding where our support lies.

ALLIES: HIGH AGREEMENT/HIGH TRUST

Those people who share our vision and who want to succeed in a way that we believe in become our allies. The strategy with allies is to treat them as if they are part of our organization, as friends, and to let them know exactly what our plans and hopes are for our function. We also need to bring allies into a discussion of our own vulnerability and doubts about what we are doing. In many ways, the way we approach allies is to put our worst foot forward. Allies can do for us many of the things that we are unable to do for ourselves. Oftentimes we have adversaries with whom communication is very difficult. We ask allies to deal directly with our adversaries in hopes of a more positive response than we ourselves are able to elicit.

In addition to identifying those people with whom we share a common vision, the second dimension has to do with trust. Allies are those people who not only share the vision but in whom we have a great deal of trust. To trust individuals in the organization is to believe they tell us the truth and are totally honest about what they see happening, including our own actions. Allies are those people to whom we feel we can tell the whole story without any concern that the knowledge will in some way come back to haunt us.

Allies appear in the upper right-hand corner of the matrix—high agreement on purpose, goals, and vision, and high trust. The basic strategy with allies is to bring them into our organization and treat them as members. Our allies may come from several groups. They may be among our customers or users who are the most successful in using the product or

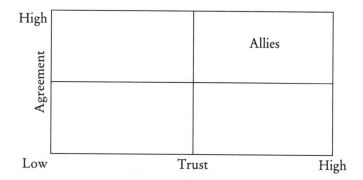

services that our group offers. We also have allies in those people above us who are very supportive of what we are doing and whom we trust to talk honestly with us about what's happening in the organization. High-level allies give us inside information to help us avoid mistakes. The third group, we hope, comprises the people who work for us. It's very difficult to have somebody in a subordinate position who has a different vision; if we also do not trust that person, the situation is intolerable.

There are a number of steps in actually managing the relationship with our allies. Each step is important in every encounter with an ally.

1. Affirm agreement on the project or the vision. It's important to be able to communicate the vision to all those around us, especially our allies. We need to tell them what our vision is, what greatness would look like for us, and in turn, reaffirm the fact that this is the direction that they support and believe in themselves. Political relationships, such as those with allies and adversaries and fence sitters, tend to be reciprocal. People who we think are our allies also view us in the same way. We are important to allies in giving support to the vision they have about where they want the organization to head. Discussing our vision, purpose, and goals with our allies is important in reaffirming this reciprocity.

2. Reaffirm the quality of the relationship.   Our allies need to know how we feel about them and what it is that they're doing that is making our relationship work so well. The honesty that exists between us needs to be reaffirmed verbally and repetitively. There is a tendency to avoid communicating positive aspects of a relationship in the midst of organizational life. It is critical to constantly say to allies, "I trust what you tell me; I feel you're honest with me, I feel I am the same with you, and that's what gives this relationship meaning."

3. Acknowledge the doubts and vulnerability that we have with respect to our vision and our projects.   Allies need to know about our adversaries and fence sitters and how we are trying to deal with them. With allies we always own up to our mistakes and the difficulties that we are engaged in. We are putting our worst foot forward.

4. Ask for advice and support.   We need our allies' confirmation on our approach, and we need their information on where other players in the game stand. Many of the people we view as opponents or difficult people in our melodrama are, in fact, opponents only through our own perception. There is a tendency based on very little data to see adversaries even where they don't exist. Our allies help us in evaluating our perceptions and in knowing the extent of the difficulty we face.

The allies most critical to us and potentially most helpful are those customers who value what we're doing and share our goal of how we want to operate. It is productive to have our customers talk about the kind of service we are giving them and how to expand it. Many groups have begun to have regular meetings with their internal customers to get feedback on how they do business, what they are doing that is appreciated, and what the customers want from them in the future. It is the equivalent of doing internally what market research has done for years in the external marketplace.

One mechanism for this is called a search conference. A department meets for a couple of days with a group composed of key customers and certain other managers who have an interest in the department. The focus is on how the department is seen by outsiders, how customers feel about the direction in which the department is headed, and what problems the customers and other outsiders will be struggling with over the next three to five years. All of this becomes vital input to understanding the nature of present and future services/products. The conference provides feedback that is hard to get any other way and also strengthens the relationship with the customer.

OPPONENTS: HIGH TRUST/LOW AGREEMENT

If we move to the lower right-hand corner of our matrix we find there are people whom we trust a great deal but who disagree with our purpose, direction, or goals.

People with whom we enjoy an honest, high-trusting relationship but who have conflicting visions, goals, or methods are our opponents. The task of the opponent is to bring out the best in us. We need to be grateful for those who oppose us in a high-trust way, for they bring the picture of reality and practicality to our plans. Their role is to challenge what we are doing in service of making us personally stronger and our strategies more effective. Sometimes when we are engaged in dialogue with an opponent who is giving us a hard time, it

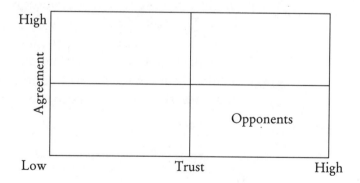

doesn't feel that way. If we ask ourselves what we want out of this discussion, it's to be right, it's to have our own way, to have confirmation in order to win. Our goal, however, is not simply to win. If all we wanted was to be right and have our own way, we would pick an arena of least resistance. To work in organizations, to have a vision, to live near the frontier, to have hope, to find meaning in our work is to pick an unsafe and difficult arena. We know that if we pick an unsafe and difficult arena, it will have brought out the best in us, and the movement toward our vision will have greater meaning for us. That is why opponents are so valuable.

It's much like playing a sport such as tennis.[6] If we ask ourselves why we play tennis and the answer is "to win," then we would look for somebody who did not know how to play the game. We would ask somebody, "Do you know how to play tennis?" and if that person said, "No, I don't," then we would say "Good. Here's a racket; you stand on the opposite side of the court, and I will hit you a ball." We would then serve the ball, the other person wouldn't know what to do with it, wouldn't hit it back, and the score would be 15-Love. We'd then tell our opponent, "Move to the right about forty feet; stand there." We would serve a second ball, our opponent would not hit it back, the score would be 30-Love, and the game would continue along these lines. We would have won every point, our opponent would have lost every point, and we would have had a wonderful afternoon.

The reality is that that's not what we look for when we engage in athletics and it is not what we need in the organization. The task of our opponent is to bring out the best in us. The better our opposition, the higher our performance. We all have the experience of playing our best against the best opponents. That's why we like tournaments, that's why we like matches, that's why we keep score. It's to test ourselves. Those

---

[6] I first heard this example from Tim Gallwey, creator of the "Inner Game" approach of learning and performance.

who fall in the category of opponents are very strong assets for our function. There are several steps in dealing with opponents that express this belief about their value to us.

1. Reaffirm the quality of the relationship and the fact that it's one based on trust.   We tell our opponents that the reason we value them is we know that they're honest with us and they'll tell us the truth, and that's what we need from them. Every step of the way.

2. State our position.   We communicate to our opponents the vision, purpose, and goals of what we're trying to do and the specifics of the project that we would like to talk to them about.

3. State in a neutral way what we think their position is.   We know they're opponents because we've already had some conversation and they have come out with a position that's different from our own. We disagree with respect to purpose, goals, and perhaps even visions. Our task is to understand their position. Our way of fulfilling that task is to be able to state to them their arguments in a positive way. They should feel understood and acknowledged by our statement of their disagreement with us.

4. Engage in some kind of problem solving.   We negotiate with our opponents the steps we will take in reaching the objectives of this particular project. What's required of us and our opponents is simply problem-solving skills, ways of looking at alternatives, ways of looking at the consequences of those alternatives. We then negotiate to the maximum extent with our opponents, knowing that because the quality of the relationship is strong, we will find some way of reaching agreement with them.

Many times people we view as adversaries are really opponents. The test is whether we trust these people. Those we trust are not adversaries but simply people who take a different position than we do. Our task is to embrace these people and to engage in dialogue and conversation with them. It is especially true if they are users of our service or our product. The people who use our service or product let us know what is needed and valuable in our product or service. It is easy for the creators of a service or product to make up their own mind about what is valuable in what they are offering and to do this in a vacuum. The essence of being customer-focused in the fulfillment of our vision is to allow customers to teach us how to do business. This takes place through a dialogue, and the most useful dialogues are with people who value and trust us but are dissatisfied with how we are serving them. It is the trusted but dissatisfied user or customer who gives us a clue to the marketplace that we do not have access to. It is very hard for us to know why people do not use our service or product and do not value what we do. It is difficult to get that information when we have ambivalence about wanting to know. In many ways, our opponents, in the form of frustrated customers, offer us a clue as to what we need to do to build more support for our function.

BEDFELLOWS: HIGH AGREEMENT/LOW TRUST

In the upper left-hand quadrant of our matrix we have bedfellows, people who are in agreement with us on how to

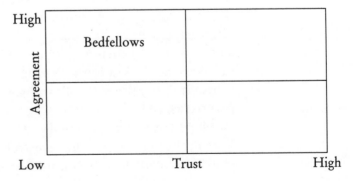

proceed but in whom we have a low to moderate amount of trust. These are people who are aligned with our vision and our goals and objectives but, when we have contact with them, don't give us the whole story. When we meet, we are strategic and careful about how much information we share. These are issues of trust, not issues of agreement. The key to approaching our bedfellows is to be true to our vision in the way that we deal with them. There is a tendency to become clever or manipulative or to go around people we don't trust. At such moments, we may be serving our ultimate purpose in terms of moving our unit ahead, but what we are doing is undermining the vision of how we want people to deal with each other inside the organization. That's why it's so critical in the vision statement to include how we want people to treat each other. That creates an accountability for us on how to deal with people such as bedfellows and adversaries. When we have less than complete trust in people, we usually think it is their fault. We talk about the fact that they don't trust us. We have evidence as to what they have done that proves them untrustworthy. Even in the face of this, we need to treat them well. The sequence for dealing with a low-trust relationship in which we have some agreement as to purpose and direction is as follows:

1. Reaffirm the agreement. We state what our purpose, our objectives, our goals for the project, perhaps even our vision are. We reaffirm the fact that our bedfellows have gone on record as supporting those things. We acknowledge and value the support we receive from them with regard to the substance of our activities.

2. Acknowledge the caution that exists. We need to put into words the fact that there is some reservation on our part as to how honest and direct the dialogue has been in the past. The key to this step is to talk about the difficulty in the relationship rather than the difficulty in the other person. At some point we have to acknowledge that we have, in fact, contributed to some of the difficulty in this relationship and that our wish is to find a way of moving ahead with the project, acknowledging the caution that exists between the two of us.

3. Be clear about what we want from bedfellows in terms of working together. We want bedfellows to be clear about where we stand. We want them to give us more than lip service; we may want them to take action that would amount to some risk on their part. We also want them to keep us well informed of what is happening around the edges of this project. The key here is for us to be clear about what we want, not in terms of the project and its goals, but in terms of how we work together.

4. Ask bedfellows to do the same. We ask our bedfellows what they want from us. The more they can express any disappointment or reservation they have in dealing with us, the better the hope there is for our future. Trust is extremely fragile in organizations; it can take years to create and moments to destroy. We want to build a trusting enough relationship with our bedfellows to get value from the support that does exist. We help this happen by encouraging bedfellows to state what they want from us. We ask them what they want from us and give them support in answering, even though we don't like what they say. The key is not to feel we have to defend ourselves. Being right doesn't help. Our intent is to help them feel understood. Bedfellows and adversaries are the most difficult relationships to manage because trust is lacking. We always have evidence of being treated unfairly. In some ways we have to forgive our bedfellows and see that their untrustworthy (through our eyes) behavior was not born of their wish to hurt us. It was most likely a result of their own vulnerability and being caught up in their own bureaucratic cycle. We forgive them their choice for caution and self-protection.

5. Try to reach some agreement with bedfellows as to how we're going to work together. We, in essence, negotiate the wants we have of the relationship. We try to create a social contract with our bedfellows as to how we're going to proceed and what we might do if things continue to be rocky. Our conversation needs to be free of threats because threats are not part of the vision that we're trying to create. The goal is a realistic discussion of how we want to work with each other and how we're going to manage this relationship. The traditional image of deal making with bedfellows is smoke-filled back rooms and closely guarded aces played at the eleventh hour. Leave this to the movies and the state capitol. Our trip is on the main street, in full view, for all to see.

FENCE SITTERS: LOW TRUST/UNKNOWN AGREEMENT

The fence sitter is someone who will simply not take a stand for or against us.

To meet with a fence sitter is to find a person who epitomizes order in the midst of chaos. Fence sitters are easy to talk to and have acquired all of the moves of interpersonal excellence. Their edges have been rounded by a series of training courses teaching the importance of good eye contact and positive reinforcement. They are good listeners, smile easily, and know how to frame issues so that apparent conflicts disappear in the understanding of alternative points of view and the need for better and more accurate data. To a fence sitter, patience and caution are next to godliness. At the end of a meeting you are never quite sure whether a decision has been

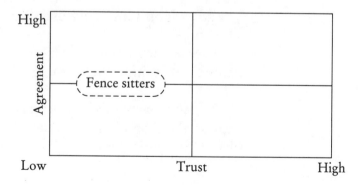

made. It seemed clear when the conversation ended, but as soon as you walk out of the room, the clarity evaporates.

At the heart of the fence sitter is doubt. The risks and uncertainty dominate the discussion. Fence-sitting is basically an editorial function. It is a triumph of form over substance. If your boss is a fence sitter, he or she likes to review and perhaps sign all written correspondence leaving the unit. Commitments made are essentially soft and filled with contingency. You learn about rules and regulations and give great attention to the positions and feelings of people not in the room.

The fence sitters present themselves as more tuned in to the "reality" of the situation than you are. The demand is to move slowly, show maturity and restraint.

The tragedy of the fence sitters' position is their (our) feelings of pessimism and helplessness. To be cautious and non-committal is an uneasy state of mind. The fence sitter is the bureaucratic prototype. To the bureaucratic mind, danger is in the foreground and opportunity is in the background. The concern is about death and failure rather than an affirmation of life. Our disappointment in fence sitters is the drain of energy we experience in their being so resigned to caution. It is hard to trust a fence sitter, and agreement evaporates with a slight breeze. This is why the fence sitter appears toward the left side, or the "low trust" side, of the continuum in the matrix.

Basically, the strategy with fence sitters is to try to smoke them out, to try to find out where they stand, to encourage them to take a position with respect to our project without slamming the door in the face of their seeming indifference. The steps look something like this:

1. State our position on the project. We state where we're headed, what our own vision, goals, and purpose are.

2. Ask where the fence sitters stand. We encourage them to express their opinion without subjecting them to the hard glare of our judgment.

3. Apply gentle pressure.   If they are true fence sitters, they will tell us they want to collect more data; they want to touch some bases and do any number of things that fence sitters do. We need to express our frustration about their neutrality. We ask for their support, and when their support is lacking, or unknown, we need to say that the fact that they are unable to take a position at this time is a disappointment to us and we would like them to take a position.

4. Encourage fence sitters to think about the issue and let us know what it would take for them to give us support.   In a sense, we want to confront them gently about their not taking a position but also leave the door open for them to come to us when it's clear where they stand on the issue.

Fence sitters are not worth a lot of energy from us. Basically, they will take positions based on their own decisions when it's safe to do so, and there's little we can do to influence them. If our boss is a fence sitter, we have the choice of viewing this as a blessing in disguise. The fact that the person either doesn't take a stand or sends us mixed signals gives us license to pursue a path of our own choosing. Our wish for our boss to take a strong supportive stand is another expression of our own wish for safety and approval—our own dependency. We have chosen our vision and, knowing we are responsible for creating this organization, have the ability to proceed without parental approval. A fence-sitting boss adds to the dangers we face, but what's the big deal? The more cautious those above us, the greater strength it requires for us to proceed. We can be grateful to those above us for giving us this opportunity.

Another basis for forgiving a fence sitter is that fence sitters are a mirror of the cautious part of ourselves. If our own wish for safety didn't run so deep, we wouldn't rail so stridently against the caution in others. Accepting the caution in others means we can accept the action in ourselves. At each moment we are complaining about the cautious behavior in those above us, one of our subordinates is somewhere having the same conversation about us. When we see this clearly, the courageous path paradoxically becomes easier for us and the fence-sitting of others becomes easier to accept.

ADVERSARIES: LOW AGREEMENT/LOW TRUST

Adversaries in some ways are the most engaging and interesting of the people that we have to deal with. They're the people that take up much of our psychic energy and our time. Adversaries are those people in the organization with whom negotiation has not worked. If we call someone an adversary, it is a position of last resort. People are bedfellows or opponents until we've tried unsuccessfully either to negotiate the relationship or to negotiate a plan of action. *People become adversaries only when our attempts at negotiating agreement and negotiating trust have failed.* Many times we identify others as adversaries when, in fact, we've had very little conversation with them and very little contact. The first basic step in dealing with adversaries is to find out if, in fact, they deserve that title. The only way to know if they deserve the title is to make direct contact with them; communicate our vision, our purpose, and our goals; ask for their support; and listen for their answer. The hardest thing about doing this is that the people we are predisposed to call adversaries are, in fact, those whom we do not trust. There's a reluctance on our part to be disclosing toward people whom we don't trust.

We create an emotional investment in our adversaries partly because, like fence sitters, they represent a side of ourselves that we are not comfortable with. Our adversaries act out of the shadow sides of our own nature. As a result, we have an investment in some people's serving as adversaries almost despite the way they behave. Often, people who are adversaries will make moves to improve the relationship with us and we're skeptical and doubtful about those moves. We rationalize them away by saying, "Well, they did that this time, but they don't really mean it." To understand our adversaries is to

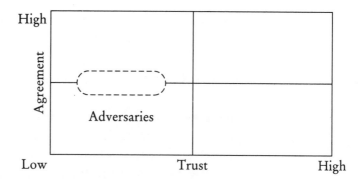

understand what it is about their behavior that we are so invested in and care so deeply about. Our essential connection to adversaries is that they behave in ways that we do not allow ourselves. The adversaries in some ways are the object of our envy, that they can act that way and get away with it when we feel that that possibility is not open to us. Adversaries become a projection of our own doubts about sides of ourselves. Our wish, then, is to convert our adversary or destroy our adversary. The irrational belief is that if I can convert or destroy my adversary, the aspect of myself that the adversary acts out will somehow be eliminated. The victory over my adversary offers the irrational hope that I will become stronger.

The way that we create our adversaries is subtle but worth examining. As an example of how this works let's take an old adversary of mine. Ed, in my eyes, seemed to have a vision that high control, high structure, caution, and smoothing things over were ways to make organizations more effective. I had trouble getting the straight story out of Ed and as a result I had little trust in him. Instead of disagreeing directly with me, he would indicate that others in the organization were the ones who had objections to what I was proposing. When I claimed aggressively that Ed was wrong—that other managers in fact told me they liked my project, Ed told me I was mistaken and that it was these other people who were not being honest with me. They were telling me what I wanted to hear. Ed and I would go round and round, and eventually the relationship deteriorated to the point at which we had as little contact as possible. Ed became for me the personification of the kind of person the organization would be better off without. I longed for the day Ed would be transferred or would lose influence. Initially, I wished for his conversion. I dreamed of the day when Ed would stop me in the hall and say, "Peter, I have been thinking about what you have been saying and have suddenly realized that you have been right all along. I do want too much control, I do want too much structure, I am too cautious, I do smooth things over, and I have not really been honest with you. It is not others who have doubts about what you are doing; the doubts I have attributed to others are really my own doubts, and I should have been more direct. I see the light and from now on you can count on me for total support." That was my dream for his conversion. Of course the conversation never happened; Ed was never converted. We remained adversaries. Not only did Ed's conversation never take place, but his influence in the organization grew. I couldn't even take pleasure in his destruction.

So what was my investment in this relationship? Strangely enough, Ed represented a side of myself that I had a hard time accepting. There is a part in each of us that is overcontrolling, overly structured, too cautious, and superficial. These qualities reflect the shadow side of our nature, and we treat them with rejection and disapproval. We do not feel entitled to act in an autocratic, structured, cautious, and superficial way. There is a side of all of us that we work hard at suppressing. Then we run across the Eds in the world, who feel absolutely entitled to act out those qualities that we strongly resent and try to deny. The reason we feel so much negative energy toward Ed is because he reminds us of our own shadow. In that sense, our view of Ed is something that we alone are responsible for. Ed is, in fact, highly controlling, highly structured, cautious, and indirect, but it is our choice to equate that with evil. We have the choice to see Ed for what he is, accept the fact that we are not going to change him, and get on with our business as best we can. Instead of moving on, we keep moving against the adversary.

We are aggressive when we are with him. We complain about him to our allies. I even write about Ed in a book like this, when I haven't seen him in years. For all I know, he may be in Central America feeding the poor and fighting for justice and equality.

Unfortunately, it doesn't work that way. The more we try to convert and pressure our adversaries, the stronger they become. Our adversaries have their vision; they are going to pursue it, and there is nothing we can do about that fact. Even if, in fact, their vision and their actions are destructive to the organization. The fact that our adversaries, by definition, are people we have no trust in means that we, of all people, are in the absolute worst position to exert influence on them. The solution is to let go of our adversaries. For our own sake and for their sake. To let go of adversaries means to stop trying to persuade them and to stop doing anything to undermine or destroy them. Our goal is to reduce the tension and threat that exist in the relationship. There are two ways to do this. One way is to completely eliminate contact with them. Why meet with them voluntarily when we know that in many ways they bring out the worst in us? If it is not possible to eliminate contact with adversaries, the second strategy is to reduce threat from them by helping them feel understood. If we can let our adversaries know that we can understand their vision and their way of getting there, it allows us both the possibility of letting go.

The strategy of letting go of our adversaries can be expressed in specific steps.

1. State our vision for our project.   We want our adversaries to be as clear as possible about what we are trying to do and why we are trying to do it. This represents our final hope that reason and good intentions will be persuasive. We usually know in our hearts that resistance from our adversaries has nothing to do with rationality, but it is worth a final shot.

2. State in a neutral way our best understanding of our adversary's position.   It is difficult to state an opposite position without making it sound unreasonable. The fear is that if we state an alternative position in a reasonable way, it will sound like we agree with that position. Restating a position does not mean we agree with it. It simply means that we can accept the fact that there are alternative views of the universe. One of the goals with an adversary is to defuse the situation. We are no longer striving for conversion or victory. The way to reduce threat is to communicate understanding. Not agreement, just understanding.

3. Identify our own contribution to the problem. If communicating understanding to adversaries seems difficult, actually telling them what we have done to move against them can seem like suicide. The fear is that if we admit to adversaries that we have lobbied against them, gone around them, discounted their position, or whispered in the ear of top management, we will be giving them ammunition to use against us. One answer to this fear is the realization that whatever damage an adversary can inflict on us has already been done. War games in organizations lose their power when they are brought into the light of day. Manipulative strategies can only thrive in darkness. When we put light on our own aggression, it serves to eliminate the weapons from both our own hands and the hands of our adversary.

We battle with our adversaries for the support of third parties. It is by living out our vision that we gain support. Owning up to our own contribution to the problem, in the midst of a bureaucratic culture, is a disarming act. It is an implied commitment on our part to cease our side of the hostilities. This is a support-building act in service of our vision. It may not win the support of our adversary, but it makes it immeasurably easier for bystanders and higher level third parties to take our side. Owning up to our own contribution to the problem, however, cannot be done as a persuasive strategy, otherwise it becomes simply a more subtle form of manipulation. We take responsibility for our part of the action because it is a statement of how we think the organization as a whole should operate.

4. End the meeting with our plans and no demand. We don't want others to be surprised by our actions, so we tell our adversary what we plan to do. Just because we are letting go of our adversary, this doesn't mean that we are letting go of our vision or objectives. This often means we have to go to another level of management to gain support. If our adversaries stand directly in our way, we may have to ask higher management to move them aside. This is a fair game, if played fairly. We only need to share this information with the adversaries. We tell them that we are going to meet with their boss, the meeting will take place on Friday at 3:00 P.M., and C.J., D.J., and P.J. will be at the meeting. Sharing our plans may make the meeting on Friday more difficult, but it is the only way to go around or over people without being manipulative.

The second part of this step is to leave the meeting without making any new demands. Letting go of our adversaries means we expect nothing from them. If making demands on adversaries could lead to some agreement, then negotiation would be possible and we would have to question whether these people were truly our adversaries. It is difficult to end the meeting without making demands. We have such a strong instinct for reciprocity that if we have owned up to our contribution to the problem and disclosed our plans, we want a like response from others. If we can't leave the meeting without making demands, then we are not ready to let go. The choice between letting go and maintaining the struggle with hopes of conversion or victory can be painful. After all, it takes a long time to nurture and develop an adversary. We have invested a lot of energy, had many conversations, mounted a series of assaults with a few partial victories. Besides, adversaries help us define who we are. It is by bouncing off others that we discover the strength of our own convictions. Adversaries also provide for us a personification of evil that makes us feel righteous by contrast. Most of all, they let us off the hook. If it weren't for them, who would we hold responsible for the shortfall of our dreams. The hardest thing to accept about adversaries is that they have friends and loved ones. How can it be that people who, in our eyes, are so misguided have loyal allies, trusted opponents, husbands and wives, and often a stature in the organization that exceeds ours? Our adversary's success in the hierarchy is living proof that there is no justice in the world and that advancement in our organization is really a triumph of form, connections, and luck (theirs) over substance, talent, and integrity (ours). Letting go of all of this isn't easy.

BOSS AS ADVERSARY.　The hardest situation of all occurs when we feel that our boss is an adversary. Working for someone we don't trust and someone who has a conflicting vision of the future is the organizational version of being on the rack. It is torture. We come to the workplace inherently distrustful of people with power over us, so our boss is a candidate for alienation even before we meet. If our boss makes some early moves that give us grief, the relationship can have a hard time recovering.

There is no real solution to the dilemma of working for an adversary. It is painful and our chances of conversion or victory are something less than slim. All we can do is pray for our boss's promotion or transfer and encourage our boss to think seriously about giving up the rat race and opening a country inn in order to be close to nature and family.

It is important to make very sure that our boss is a true adversary. The fact that our boss has power over us triggers the nonassertive side of ourselves and makes us a little too ready to conclude that negotiation has failed. We might as well negotiate hard with an adversarial boss because we have little to lose. I have seen many people who have prematurely concluded that their bosses were adversaries without ever expressing what they wanted from them. The primary choices open to us are to act as if the boss is only an opponent or bedfellow, with negotiation a possibility, or to leave and look for peace in another department.

Some people talk a lot about "managing your boss," but what they really are suggesting is manipulating your boss. You hear things like we should work to make bosses look good, make them think it was their idea, show them that what we propose is in their best interest, and on and on. These "techniques" usually come back to haunt us. What makes us think that bosses are such fools that they don't realize what is happening? We generally know when others are playing games with us; what makes us think that we are any more perceptive than those around us? We need to play it above board with our boss, otherwise we will have undermined our own vision and made progress following a path we don't believe in. And for what purpose—advancement, power, self-esteem, pride, hard cash, and a corner office? Well, now that you mention it, that sounds pretty good.

SUBORDINATE AS ADVERSARY.   When you have a subordinate you don't trust, more torture takes place, but this time someone else is on the rack. Having an adversarial subordinate is frustrating for us, but it is a nightmare for the other person. The solution here also is to let go, but in the case of subordinates, we ask them to leave. The first choice, of course, is to keep negotiating and try to rebuild some trust in the relationship. Luckily in most cases this will work out. We can live with subordinates who are opponents, fence sitters, and even bedfellows. The goal is to move the subordinate into one of these categories by building trust or agreement. When this fails, the only compassionate act is to ask the subordinate to opt out. The thought of having someone whom you don't trust and who doesn't share your vision represent your unit to your customers is intolerable. So let go of the subordinate. Do it gently, giving the person support and perhaps even an outplacement counselor, but get on with it.

Looking at the choices we have in building support, our goal is to move people toward the upper right-hand quadrant of the matrix — to increase trust and agreement. It makes sense to spend most of our time with current allies and to seek new ones. A well-articulated vision statement and authentic behavior are the best way to find the support. Our second level of energy goes to our opponents. They teach us about the marketplace for our ideas and help us get our act together. They also tend to speak well of us when we are not in the room. People will listen to them because it is known that our opponents do not agree with us on everything. The third order of priority is bedfellows. We want their support and it takes rather persistent contact to maintain a fragile level of trust. Fence sitters become a passing fancy because they are finally going to take a position based on breezes outside our control. As for adversaries, two more meetings are all that are required. One meeting to try to negotiate trust or agreement one more time. Then one meeting to confess and say goodbye. If, despite all this eloquent prose, you choose to keep on trying to convert or destroy your adversaries, your next book should be *Winning Through Intimidation* or *You Are What You Eat*.

BALANCING AUTONOMY

AND DEPENDENCE:

PEACE WITH THOSE AROUND YOU

To realize our vision in an organizational setting, we need the support of those around us. Users and suppliers need our unit, bosses need subordinates, colleagues need peers. The need for interdependence and cooperation is ideally expressed by the idea that we are all partners in creating this business. Mars candy company and others call their employees "associates" as a way of expressing the sentiment that they are all in this together, roughly as equals. Moving toward an entrepreneurial contract and a definition of self-interest as contribution and integrity calls for us to act as equals even when we deal with those above us whose offices are palatial and whose windows overlook the Golden Gate Bridge. Empowering ourselves as middle managers means putting our survival in our own hands and requires that we act as interdependent partners in each encounter.

A major source of interference to our empowerment is our own dependency. This chapter explores the wish inside all of us to place our survival in someone else's hands. The entrepreneurial choice for autonomy and empowerment is well served by understanding what we do to keep ourselves in psychological bondage.

The basic patriarchal contract asks that we maintain high control, revere external authority, and be willing to make sacrifices for the good of the organization. As subordinates we may have doubts about the autocratic nature of the contract and yet we agree to live within it. A part of each of us believes that strong, clear authority is the only realistic antidote to chaos, unpredictability, and self-indulgence. We are conditioned from the beginning to treat people who have power over us with lot of attention and respect. This yearning for external control is an expression of our dependency. Dependency, the belief that our survival is in someone else's hands, is realistic in our early years and becomes an issue we have to deal with the rest of our lives. This chapter is about dependency, how it evolves, the forms that it takes, when it makes sense, how it can get in the way, how to get past it, and ultimately how to live with the feeling, even at work, that our lives are our own.

The dependent part of ourselves is reluctant to risk or to take responsibility for the future of our unit. This is becoming a critical issue for many companies because of their commitment to becoming leaner and more participative. Many managers, increasingly aware of the price we pay for too many controls, have had the belief that if some of those controls were removed, a tremendous amount of positive energy in service of the organization would be released. While in many instances this has happened, too often our attempts at giving people more responsibility have been unwelcomed and met with persistent reluctance. Many managers have tried repeatedly to open the door of participation to their people, only to find them reluctant to walk through it. I described earlier a major project with supermarket store managers to give them total responsibility to manage their own stores. About 20 percent of the managers took the responsibility and ran with it; about 50 percent of the managers cautiously tested our sincerity and then over a period of six months began to make their own decisions. The frustrating part of the effort was that the other 30 percent absolutely refused to take the reins. They clutched tightly to their dependency and continued to complain that top management did not really mean it, they were not given enough people or resources to really do the job, and the unique characteristics of their particular location made our efforts at participative management unreasonable.

This reluctance of people to claim their autonomy takes many forms. Every time we set up a task force, the first question that arises is "How much authority do we have?" When we reassure them that they do have some control, they keep testing it. The most popular fictional character in organizational life is "they." We must be in love with "they," because we talk about "they" all the time. They won't let us do this, they shoot messengers, they care more about form than substance, they don't want to hear problems, they just want solutions. They won't make up their minds, they don't provide the leadership we need, they force groups to compete with each other, they don't want to hear the truth — and so it goes. All the talk about "they" is the way our dependency gets expressed. In twenty years of conducting training workshops in organizations, I have never once had the right people in the room. The first question a group of middle managers asks is "Has top management been through this workshop?" If the answer is no, the group replies, "How do you expect us to try these things if they are not supported and rewarded by our bosses?" If top management has been through the workshop, the reply is "Well, they may have been through the workshop, but they are not really using the skills." If top management is going through the workshop, they declare, "This is fine for us, but the group that really needs it is the next level down."

The chorus of nonresponsibility needs to be understood. To blame the lack of entrepreneurial behavior solely on the unwillingness of managers to give up control is only a partial explanation. If we seriously want to transform organization cultures, we have to confront and understand our own wish to be dependent and to see what choices we have.

POLITICAL SCRIPTS

Our dependency is closely tied to the way we choose to be political. One of the basic tenets of this book is that negative politics is a direct outgrowth of the fact that we give too much power to the people around and above us. Our fear that power will be used against us in a destructive way leads us to be indirect and manipulative. We use indirect strategies as a way of coping with our frustration at not getting our way. We defend manipulation with our claim that it is a jungle out there and authenticity would be suicidal and a choice for unemployment and poverty. The problem arises when we become so accustomed to negative politics that we continue to use it even when the external dangers have disappeared. Each of us has developed over the years a patterned way of dealing with powerful people. This is our political script. Our script is an influence strategy that we bring to the party almost independent of who our boss is or what kind of organizational environment we are working in. It is by understanding these scripts that we eventually are able to choose them instead of being controlled by them.

As with many things in our life, the origins of our script began very early. We had to deal with the helplessness of being very small children surrounded by very large adults called parents or guardians. For many of us the first six months of life went quite smoothly. All we had to do was cry, and the organization (our family) mobilized itself to figure out and satisfy our needs. We lived as kings and queens, bellowing our demands for these large, powerful adults to examine each of our orifices, to identify the source of our discomfort, and to fix it. We had all the skills we needed to get the approval, attention, safety, and control that we wanted. It may be that our frustration now stems from having peaked too early.

At about six months of age, however, something changed, and we never have recovered. They started to say no to us. As we became mobile and adventuresome, we were confronted with the dangers of stoves, stairs, and pointed objects. We also developed a destructive capability toward valuable possessions placed on low coffee tables. Being told no at the onset of our first moves toward freedom begins what is called the socialization process. Socialization is a system of restraints designed to give us the skills to move safely and cooperatively within society. As children we are realistically dependent. Our survival is in fact in someone else's hands. The good news is that we are being taken care of; the bad news is that others have their own ideas about how to take care of us. Our dilemma as children is how to live with the parental restraints and still get what we want. Our needs for attention, approval, safety, and control only intensify, and at some point, no matter how loved we are, our parents' response falls short. Our parents or guardians, being human and imperfect, in some ways disappoint us. Confronted with our dependency and our frustration, we begin to develop strategies on how to get what we want from people who have power over us. These strategies, indirect by necessity, become our political scripts. These scripts are created and honed in the early years at home, are developed even further in school, and finally are brought into the workplace. Bosses become our surrogate parents, and bosses recreate for us in our adult years many of the feelings and dilemmas our parents created for us in our early years. The dependency we express toward our bosses is often based on habitual responses that go back a long way. Later we will examine these scripts in some detail, but let's go back to our childhood and how we calculate to get what we want.

At the age of six months, we are not only faced with learning the meaning of the word no, but we also begin to discover that our parents have needs too. They want some recognition from us! The first words they teach us are their names: Mommy, Daddy, and sometimes Uncle Harry or Aunt Alice (if we have single parents with live-in partners). This is getting to be a real problem. They are not only putting restraints on our freedom, but they want something in return for their love and affection. This introduces the process of interpersonal deal making. "If you want me to give you what you want, you had better respond in kind." Our first response to this new turn of events is to revert to techniques that have been successful in the past—we yell our heads off. If this doesn't work, we try a new strategy—guilt. We hold our breath until our face turns red, then blue. The message is, "Look what you are doing to me. If you don't give me what I want I will threaten you with my own destruction." Despite the fact that our parents have a weight advantage of 110 to 180 or more pounds, the battle for dominance and independence has begun. And on roughly an equal basis. From this point on the strategies become more sophisticated and, at the risk of oversimplifying, fall into one of two categories: imitation or rebellion.

If you are around kids you see them practice their imitative moves constantly. If you are around kids, you see them constantly role playing adult scenes.

Child as wife [mop in hand]: Well, dear, have a nice day at the office.

Child as husband: You have a nice day at home. [This was a long time ago.]
[leaving with papers in hand]

Child as wife: What time will you be home tonight?

Child as husband: Five-thirty.

Child as wife: That's what you said last night and you got home at eight o'clock.

Child as husband: It was not eight; it was seven fifty-one.

Child as wife: Well, tonight I expect you home by five-thirty.

Child as husband: I'll try. [Said with little conviction.]

The statement the children are making through their rehearsal and imitation is "Now that we are like them, they will give us what we want." This imitation is a fundamental influence strategy that persists even into the workplace. We see a great deal of effort to imitate and fit into the culture on the part of employees, especially early in their career. If I imitate my boss, operate according to his or her style, it is a powerful demonstration of loyalty and commitment and will surely increase my chances of winning approval.

The opposite strategy to imitation is rebellion. Rebellion is as dependent an act as imitation. When I rebel, I am determined to do the opposite of what you expect of me. Your expectations are still driving my behavior, but in the opposite direction. Rebellion demands attention, involvement, and concern. If you want to see the face of rebellion, just ask a teenager to clean her room and keep it clean for twenty-four hours. In most organizations we don't have to deal too much with direct rebellion. People who have chosen this path usually get screened out in the recruitment process or within the first year or two. The only place that explicit rebellion is tolerated in organizations is at occasional retirement parties. There is often one employee, well known for his antimanagement attitudes, who as guest speaker at a retirement party, roasts the organization with humor and much laughter.

There are certainly more options than simply imitation or rebellion. What is key is the concept that we use our behavior as a hidden bargain with people who have power over us. This act of manipulating our behavior as a form of exchange is our dependency made visible. As we get older and move from dependency to autonomy, we become more comfortable acting in more authentic ways and living with the consequences of how people in power may feel about it. The child in us thinks that what we need for our survival is the attention, approval, protection, and territory/control bestowed on us by those above. The alternative is to realize that although those things are gratifying, there are deeper things we want that we can only provide for ourselves, namely, meaning, a feeling of contribution and service, integrity, and mastery. Constantly seeking the approval of those above us is a form of outdated dependency that keeps placing the handcuffs on ourselves and compels us to be attracted by indirect, negatively political actions. Constantly resisting influence from above has the same effect.

It is important for us to understand what form our own political behavior takes. What follows are some common ways we indirectly go after what we want. These political scripts in and of themselves are not a problem; in fact, they can become our strengths. The risk is they often become subtle ways we keep ourselves from taking responsibility for our actions and for the organization. The political scripts get us in trouble when we use our behavior as a form of implicit barter. We are making a deal that if I treat you this way, you will give me what I want. Strategic, script-oriented bartering then replaces direct, authentic communication. Positive politics requires direct communication of wants, feelings, hopes, disappointments, and doubts. Direct contact is especially required in dealing with people who have power over us, even though the risks are greater.

I have identified eight political scripts that give most of us something to identify with. These scripts become a problem when we use them as the basis for a hidden bargain: "Now that I have behaved this way, you will be compelled to give me what I want." It is a use of my behavior as influence strategy, and it lays the groundwork for disappointment. Hidden bargains involve our unexpressed wants, and often people are driven away from us because we overuse the very behavior designed to elicit their support. You are welcome to add to this list or combine some scripts. As you go through the explanations, pick the one or two that are your favorites. If you think you engage in all of them, you are being a fence sitter. Based on extensive research (I interviewed three people on a bus ride from Bayonne, New Jersey, to King of Prussia, Pennsylvania) here are the eight political scripts:

Rescue	Rebel
Look good	Be aggressive
Be pleasing	Be formal
Withdraw	Be superrational

RESCUE.   The rescuer deeply believes that the path to power, influence, and gaining some control over the situation is to save other people's lives. If we help others with their problem, they will give us what we want. The key to our own feeling of entitlement is to have established a track record of service and compassion that will erase others' disappointment or anger with us. It is a way of finessing our way out of others' negative feelings. Look at how much we have done for others. Look at how we have helped them in their time of need. Look how they can always count on us to pay attention to their difficulties. Look at the personal sacrifice we have willingly made. Now will they give us what we want? The rescuer needs a victim. Someone to help. Like all other forms of dependency, this one is a way of blunting and neutralizing the power other people have over us. To understand the rescuer inside of us, ask which of our parents or guardians we took care of and how we did it.

As rescuers we need someone else in trouble to feel good about ourselves; we need someone to save. We also tend to see other people as fragile and needing to be rescued. Seeing others as fragile and needing to be rescued is, like all other forms of dependency, a projection of our own feelings about ourselves. Underneath the pride we take in our lifesaving ability is our own sense of fragility, our own need for someone to appear who can protect us and get us out of trouble. If we feel that there is no one around who can provide safety for us, then we do the next best thing; we say to others, especially those with power over us, "Don't worry about it; I'll take care of you; you can count on me. And after I have solved problems that you have created, then will you give me what I want?"

Profile: Rescuer
- Telltale Signs:
    High sensitivity to others' discomfort.
    Willingness to postpone getting what we want.
    Belief that our rewards will come in the next life, the next job, the next performance review.

- Side of Ourselves We Deny:
    Our own need to be one up.

- Price We Pay:
    We become cynical, disappointed that other people are never grateful enough.

LOOK GOOD.   If we do everything right, others will never find reasons to hold us back. Our perfection, looking good at all times, even when it is not true, is our ticket to entitlement. Because we are well behaved, a good and outstanding employee, meet our goals, behave, respect authority without being solicitous, we have a right to make demands and receive our just rewards. Being perfect, others can never find fault with us. We are a living advertisement in *Gentleman's Quarterly* or *Working Woman* magazine. We have clear objectives for what we do. We have well-defined milestones for each step of the way. We have a filing system that never fails us. Our presentations are crisp and very rational. We have no problems, only opportunities. We are never surprised. No matter what happens, it was part of the plan. The plea of the perfect person is "Now that I have become a replica of exactly what you wish me to be, will you give me what I want?" To be perfect is to make no errors, to provide a smooth, mirrorlike finish to the world. Since others can find no fault with us, we have softened their power.

Profile: Look Good

- Telltale Signs:
    High standards, loudly proclaimed.
    Wonder what the big deal is about overachieving.

Note: Neale Capp, a friend and colleague, was extremely helpful in creating these profiles. For his help, I agreed to declare him free from any of these forms of dependency.

Quietly judge others who don't meet the standards. "I don't expect anything more from you than I expect from myself."

All work clothes are gray and blue so that mismatching is technically impossible.

Clean desk, clean appearance, clean car (even after a long trip with small children).

- Side of Ourselves We Deny:
  Our self-doubt and vulnerability.

- Price We Pay:
  We are slow to learn from mistakes we never make; we are exhausted from never letting down.

BE PLEASING.   If we feel that people will give us what we want if we make them happy, we have the potential to use pleasing as a political strategy. As children we decide early in the game that making a parent unhappy can lead to disastrous consequences. It is important to smile for Daddy. We please others by smiling a lot, even when we don't feel like smiling. We have seen the consequences of our parents' anger on others and we don't want that to happen to us. Often pleasers have a brother or sister who chose a more adventurous path who might have been aggressive or rebellious. Aggressive and rebellious strategies are for those who are willing to take their lumps to get what they want. Pleasing is a way of getting what we want, paying what seems at the time like the minimum price. We apologize easily. If we make mistakes, it was because we didn't understand the instructions or were careless and it won't happen again. We would never admit that we didn't want to do it in the first place. We are nice to be around, use humor a lot to connect with people. At work, our main concern is to be like those we work for. We want to know how to fit in, to be of service, and when we hear in a performance review that people like us have very good interpersonal skills, it is a dream come true. Now that we have been indiscriminately nice to people we don't really care about, now do we get what we want? As pleasers we believe that if we make strong, explicit demands on others, we will never get what we want and will eventually be punished.

Profile: Pleaser

- Telltale Signs:
  Smile, smile, smile.
  Nodding head when others are talking.
  When others ask, "How did you like the play, Mrs. Lincoln," we say, "Fine, thank you."

- Side of Ourselves We Deny:
  Our own conceit, arrogance, and contempt.

- Price We Pay:
  Our own cup is empty; feeling of giving to others what we ourselves can't get.

WITHDRAW.   Withdrawing as a political strategy means we see the world as a particularly dangerous place. People with power over us are making demands and expectations that it will be impossible to satisfy. Why play a losing game? For our survival, we will play a private game. Distance is the key to survival and getting what we want. Feelings, thoughts, facial expressions, anything that may in subtle ways get us involved over our head are things to be avoided. Confrontation and conflict are painful, and the way we avoid them is not to be around. We leave early in the morning and come back at night. When others ask where we were, we say "out" or "at work" or "doing some things." The response is designed to discourage further inquiry. The life stance is that we can take care of ourselves. The way that we will get what we want from others is by not bothering them. Spending time alone is the preferred strategy. Being on our own gives us a feeling of control over our actions and, more important, it frees us from the feeling of being controlled. Withdrawing is a strategy for achieving our independence.

At work, in the face of powerful people we are quiet, somewhat hard to read, and live with the thought that difficult issues are always better dealt with at a later time — a time when we can have more control over the outcome. When others complain about our withdrawal, our defense is that we are not bothering anyone else, so why don't they quit hassling us? Since we don't bother them and we take care of ourselves, why don't others give us what we want?

Profile: Withdrawer

- Telltale Signs:
  Expressionless face, neither a smile nor a frown.
  Silence in meetings.
  Minimal sharing of information.
  Little humor.
  Offense to no one.
  A feeling of waiting for something.
  When confronted, an unenthusiastic agreement to do better next time.

- Side of Ourselves We Deny:
  Our wish for intimacy.

- Price We Pay:
  Loneliness.

REBEL. All of us are uneasy and cautious about authority. As rebels, resisting authority, breaking the rules, and creating rules of our own are the ways we unintentionally cement our dependence. On the surface we are claiming our independence. By making our own rules and consciously violating the norms and rules of others, we declare ourselves free and our own person. Underneath the surface independence lies the fact that we need others' rules and structure to give us something to stand against. Our identity exists only in contrast to the constraints and authority of others. Our identity does not come from within but comes from response to events from without. By the time we reach the age of employment, much of our early, more adolescent rebellion has been dampened. If we were too rebellious, no one would hire us. There is a natural weeding out of the superrebel. But the instinct remains. We live in sharp contrast to the pleaser and withdrawer. We love conflict and disagreement. The gift we have for others is our willingness to engage. The outlet for our resisting way of dealing with authority is our embrace of democratic values and participative management.

The positive element of this form of dependency is the affirmation of individual rights. We become a useful critic of the organization and although we may express our criticism too aggressively, we are often voicing the thoughts of the more cautious and that is our gift.

Profile: Rebel

- Telltale Signs:
    Clothes are unique but acceptable.
    Style is engaging and fun to be around.
    Last in, first out at meetings.
    Technically bright and talented enough to survive.

- Side of Ourselves We Deny:
    Our wish for approval.

- Price We Pay:
    Despair from never committing.

BE AGGRESSIVE.   In many ways aggression is the most direct way of pursuing what we want. The joy of dealing with an aggressive person is that we know where that person stands. Aggression is the ultimate act of entitlement. It is the pursuit of power, even at the expense of other people's wants and needs. It is the belief that the world is a primitive place where only the strong survive. It is the child looking at a world of large, powerful people and coming to the conclusion that the only way one can get what one wants is to go after it. It is the act of reaching and grabbing. It is also keenly aligned with the cultural prototype of the American, independent John Wayne persona. Alone, surrounded by hostile forces, focused on clear goals. A train hurtling through the night.

There is the softer, more vulnerable side of the aggressive choice. It comes from the child's view of the dominant parent. The child experiences the control of the parent and says, in effect, I will be like you and then you will give me what I want. To be aggressive and grab control tightly is a response to the inner feeling that if we are not careful, control will be lost. If we weren't afraid of losing control, why would we hold onto it so tightly?

Underneath the aggressive act is the fear that there is nothing really to hold onto. This is the common fear that lies within each of us—we each just make different choices as to how to respond to the fear. Do we please others, rescue them, withdraw from them, behave perfectly, or look for control and dominance in each situation?

In organizations, aggressive people are viewed with deep ambivalence. When it comes to getting a job done, we want people to leap over obstacles, drive through walls, be persistent, focused, and single-minded. At the bottom levels of the ladder, we reward aggression and dominance. As we move up the organization, the rules change, and we want people to smooth out. We want their rough edges to be rounded and for them to treat other people more gently. The dominant behavior that is applauded early in life gets restrained later in life. The independent controlling action that gets rewarded early in our career is fought and resisted later in our career.

Profile: Aggressive

- Telltale Signs:

Scars and bruises.

Energetic, easy to understand.

Send birthday and Christmas cards to each subordinate as a major employee relations strategy.

Never give performance reviews.

"Touchy/feely stuff" causes hives.

- Side of Ourselves We Deny:
  Our wish to be dependent and controlled.

- Price We Pay:
  Isolation. End game disappointment.

BE FORMAL.　Many of us learned early in the action that the way to get what we want is to be formal and polite and to have a strong belief in rules, policies, and procedures. We grew up in households that were very structured and orderly. A family in which people knew their place and shared the belief that the success of the family and the security of the future would somehow be ensured if we treated each other with respect, dignity, decorum, and also distance. Being formal and polite is a way of showing sensitivity to others, and it is also a strategy for getting our way by making sure our actions and apparent motives are unimpeachable. It is the child saying to the parents, "I am living by your rules; I treat you the same way you treat each other. Since I follow the rules, on the surface, as if I truly believed in them, now will you give me what I want?"

At the heart of the belief in formality as a political strategy is the silent contract that we will not raise difficult issues with others if they will not raise difficult issues with us. The formality serves to postpone or avoid conflict. To be formal, not to raise difficult issues with each other, is based on the fear that lurking underneath the politeness of our interaction is a dangerous sea of feelings, wishes, impulses, and demands.

If this underworld were exposed, we would be in trouble. We would lose control, and everything we have worked so hard to create would be threatened. Each political strategy is a variation of our efforts to gain some control over our lives to limit our vulnerability in the face of powerful forces outside ourselves. That is the dilemma of the child: "Since you will not give me what I want of your own free will, how can I go about getting my needs met in the face of the power you have over me?" It is inevitable that the expectations we have of our parents or guardians will at some point be unfulfilled, and it is inevitable that we will have to develop ways to overcome that disappointment and get what we want in our own way. In a family situation that values structure and propriety and is very conscious of appearances, a strategy of being formal, still, and polite is a logical choice.

The transfer of formal behavior from the family to the school to the organization is an easy transition. The essence of most organizations' efforts to be well managed are based on a strong belief in rules, policies, and procedures. That this belief in procedures flies in the face of the entrepreneurial spirit is beside the point. The desire for control and structure is often much stronger than the desire for performance.

If our strategy of influence has been to be formal, structured, and geared to avoiding conflict, working in a large, bureaucratic system is like going home again.

Profile: Be Formal

- Telltale Signs:
  Desk piled with papers, all neatly stacked.
  Like to say "sir" to people with authority, even women.
  Photo of family in dress clothing taken by Weston, Steiglitz, or Karsh Studios.

- Side of Ourselves We Deny:
  Our internal confusion and chaos.

- Price We Pay:
  Loss of love, passion, and excitement.

BE SUPERRATIONAL.   In a culture that treats science and rationality as a religion, choosing a strategy of superrationality as a path to getting our way is a logical choice.

Rationality is a belief in the world of ideas and abstractions. When we are faced with confusion or disappointment, our way of coping with it is by trying to understand it. If we can understand what is happening to us, we don't feel so bad about it. When we are confronted with difficult issues, unreasonable demands, complicated, messy situations that occur every day in organizational life, our response is to intellectualize the issue. Someone says, "The manufacturing department is furious that the design for the automatic dispenser is not completed." Our superrational response is "Don't they understand that the seven-stage process for integrating the variant demands of the multipurpose, multisite dispenser has critical requirements that demand the integration of a variety of subcomponents, each with its own critical path and its own unique constellation of inherent forces?" Right. Each complicated problem to the superrational is a theory waiting to be understood and expressed. Rationality demands data, it needs data, it loves data. The rational political strategy holds that data do exist to solve the current problem.

In the face of conflict or stress, the rational response is to look for more data and to study the situation further. This deep belief in rationality expresses a great distrust in the intuitive and nonrational side of ourselves. There is, of course, great value in rationality, but the risk is the denial or blindness to events that cannot be completely explained or for which the data are subjective. As superrational people we base the claim to our demands on reason and logic and the belief that if others cannot prove us wrong, then they have to give us what we want. We will deny the fact that rationality can be simply a strategy to get what we want from powerful people — a political strategy — because there is no concrete evidence to support such a claim.

You can tell when you are dealing with a superrational person by noticing that when you start to get close to a sensitive issue or an issue that has fuzzy elements, the subject subtly shifts to other situations or concepts that drain the emotion and take you to a higher level of abstraction. A discussion about a problem between manufacturing and engineering becomes a discussion about the economic forces impacting your industry or your company and how top management has played a key role in keeping this problem from being resolved.

The fear of the superrational is that the world is unpredictable, unexplainable, and therefore dangerous. It is out of control and that fact leaves us feeling helpless and unable to get what we need. When we cope with the feeling of helplessness through explanations, data, and abstractions, and do this as an influence strategy, we are enacting a superrational strategy.

Profile: Superrational

- Telltale Signs:
  Degree in engineering or accounting.
  Very successful.
  The book *Lives of a Cell* by Lewis Thomas changed our life.
  Someday want to teach.
  Arrive early at meetings.
  Elaborate filing systems close at hand.

- Side of Ourselves We Deny:
  Our emotionality.

- Price We Pay:
  We lose contact with own feelings. It's hard to make intimate connections.

THE RIGHT USE OF SCRIPTS

These political scripts only get in our way when the use of them becomes an expression of our dependency. Using rationality, pleasing, or rescuing as a strategy for getting what we want from people with power is inherently manipulative and indirect. It becomes a hidden bargain: "Now that I have pleased you, now that I have rescued you, now that I have given you data and logic—now will you give me what I want?" It is the misuse of these scripts that can get us in trouble.

When we act out the script simply and purely for its own sake, the script becomes our strength and is a way of declaring our autonomy and our individuality. "I please you, I rescue you, I explain the world, because I love to do it for its own sake and after all these years, that is what I do best." Our script becomes an expression of what we have to offer. We offer it with no expectation of reward. It is the dependent child in us that complains, "After all I have done for you, look at how you have disappointed me." When other people's actions become an excuse for our actions, our dependency is in full bloom. All of our efforts in others' behalf, our pleasing, rescuing, and research, were done for the effect they would have on others, not for their own sake or because they were something we, and we alone, chose to do. When our script becomes our choice, we are at that moment responsible for our actions, we claim our autonomy, we are pursuing an entrepreneurial path.

Standing for our own autonomy, choosing our own script, conscious of but uncontrolled by the expectation of our surrogate parents (bosses) becomes a positive political act, especially in the midst of the bureaucratic cultures in which we work.

When we become conscious of our favorite scripts, the tendency at first is to try to change them. We make resolutions to try to stop pleasing, rescuing, withdrawing and being so aggressive. These resolutions ultimately fail, and we "regress." We should be grateful that our self-conversion fails. To extinguish resolutely a script in ourselves is a futile act of self-denial. It is a denial of what makes us unique and a denial of the very thing we have to contribute. The goal is to stop using the script for effect or as an influence strategy. No bargaining allowed. Using our behavior as currency for achieving influence is a dependent, subtly manipulative act, even if it works. It is based on the belief that the only way we will be successful is by maneuvering our way into prominence. It is based on the belief that our bosses are somewhat foolish and gullible and can be handled by our attempts at "I'll use this technique to bring you over to my side." The reality is that our bosses are no more foolish or gullible than we are.

We know when someone is dependently seeking our approval and so do our bosses. The alternative is to recognize fully that we are not in this job simply to seek our bosses' approval. Our bosses are not our parents. The key to our survival is not in their hands. The key to our survival is in the quality and integrity of the work that we do. It is in the quality and integrity of the way we manage our work relationships. The approval of our bosses will come and go with the rising and falling of the tides, and the rising and falling of the fortunes of our unit and function. Putting tremendous energy into other-directed, script-oriented strategies is a self-defeating investment. We all have our scripts; it is important that we know what they are so that we can choose them; they express who we are as individuals. They are the form that our contribution to the business takes, and this is what gives them value. The task is to be aware of how the scripts operate to reinforce our dependency and to let go of that use of the scripts. Political scripts, at this stage of our lives, are not there for our personal gain. They are there for our personal expression and contribution.

USEFUL DEPENDENCY

Having spent so much time discussing the evils of dependency, let me be realistic for a moment. Each of us is dependent on other people. The fact that we need other people is what makes us human. In fact, organizations serve the useful role of bringing us together, providing a vehicle to engage in cooperative activity, and giving us a sense of community. A big part of the fun of work is the process of creating something jointly with others. We also need bosses and subordinates. Coordinating a large number of people requires that we have several different levels of authority and that some people should have power over others. As a result we are dependent on bosses and that will never change. Dependency is realistic and functional in certain ways. What follows are some ways in which we are appropriately dependent along with the risks to us if we carry these useful forms of dependency too far.

NAMING THE GAME.   Unless we are at the very top of the organization, we need someone to tell us what game we are going to play. We need one voice from the top telling what business we are in, what the basic givens and groundrules are for pursuing that business. We live within a given structure and mission statement, and we need those at the top to decide on basic goals. We need clarity on how fast we should grow and what kind of financial performance will keep the organization stable and healthy. We carry this need for basic direction too far if we also ask those above us to create a vision of greatness for our own function. Our vision of a preferred future for our unit needs to be our own creation. We decide what kind of unit we will become, all the time operating within the framework and limits offered from above.

CONFIRMATION.   We are dependent on those above and around us to confirm and validate that what we are doing is contributing something of value. We want to satisfy our customers and bosses because they represent the marketplace for our service/ product, and the basic purpose of our unit is to fulfill a real need. We are very dependent on feedback from others to let us know when we are doing something right. Confirmation lets us know that our own judgment about what we are doing has some external validity. The singer needs the applause. The wish for applause goes too far when we let it become essential for our own self-esteem. Self-esteem comes from our own decisions to risk, to act, to change, to live our life. No one else has the power to make us feel good about ourselves. If we basically look to others to answer our questions about our own worth, we are trapped. We need from others validation about choices we alone have made.

CONTACT.   We need to feel connected to those around us. All of us need a certain level of intimacy, and work is a great place to find it. The way we make contact with each other is all over the map, but the need is universal, especially given the complexity of life in an organization. We stay where we are and put up with incredible obstacles in order to maintain close relationships. Our dependency on others for contact is good for us and glue to the organization, particularly in hard times. Our need for others goes too far when we allow ourselves to be swallowed or enveloped. If our need for intimacy is too great, we lose our sense of self. Some of us fear abandonment so intensely that we lose the ability to stand up to another. When others' approval, even our boss's becomes so important to us that we deny our own position, our dependency has become our enemy.

TEMPORARY PROTECTION.   Even though our deep wish to find a safe path can never be fulfilled, it is realistic to expect those above us to shield us and intervene in our behalf from time to time. As a new and naive employee at Exxon I remember saying no too bluntly to the wrong person. The only thing standing between me and the street was my manager. He set up a meeting with the offended vice president and coached me before the meeting. At the meeting, the vice president looked at me and said, "Block, when you are in the oil fields and they tell you to grab the wrench and hit the tower, by God, you grab the wrench and hit the tower. Do you get my meaning?" Thanks to the sophisticated coaching of my manager, I said, "Yes . . . sir," and kept the wolf from the door a little longer. We have a right to expect this kind of help from our bosses, and they usually want to give it to us. We get into trouble when we expect the organization to give us any long-term guarantees.

To be cautious, political, and approval seeking because we think it is the long-run safe path is a foolish strategy.

LEARNING.   We are also dependent on our bosses, colleagues, and customers to teach us the business. There is a strong correlation between learning and performing. There is strength in taking the stance of being a lifelong learner. The hard part is being able to see our mistakes clearly and to forgive ourselves for making them. The only downside risk to our need to learn occurs if we use it as an excuse for not acting.

AUTONOMY AND INTERDEPENDENCE

Giving such emphasis to individual autonomy often seems like an argument against interdependence and our need for each other. This is not the intent. Our belief is that teamwork and interdependence are most effective when people choose to work together from a position of individual strength. I like the image that it takes two whole eggs to make an omelette. If we choose to be in a relationship because we are afraid that we cannot make it on our own, it puts a terrible strain on the relationship. Even though we all need to be dependent at times, if our dependency is a persistent and steady diet, it creates resentment and a set of unrealized expectations. We claim our autonomy when we accept the fact that the things that are essential to our survival are the things we have to create for ourselves. This is the mind-set that allows relationships to survive.

When we choose to work in an organizational setting, we are deciding that connectedness and interdependence are essential to us. Why else would we put up with all those meetings? Our desire for interdependence is expressed by the part of the vision statement that defines how we want people to treat each other. How we treat each other is as important to the organization's success as the focus on economic goals and accomplishments. Of the hundreds of vision statements I have heard, I cannot think of one that did not in some way call for love, compassion, or teamwork. Being autonomous gives us the freedom to choose whom we want to be with and how we want to be with them.

FINDING PEACE WITH THE BOSS

Even though our dependency is at times appropriate, we are still faced with the dilemma of how to move toward an increasing sense of autonomy. Our political script gets activated and we engage in negative politics as a response to situations in which people have power over us. We are constantly in the process of working out how we handle authority. Our tendency is to manage those under us in the way that we want to be managed. Saying that we have to have tight control of those under us because we ourselves are tightly controlled is as much our wish as it is our complaint. Our boss symbolizes power to us, and it is by reexamining our expectations of our boss that we discover our own autonomy and entrepreneurial potential.

Our wish for approval, attention, recognition, and safety from our boss is similar in kind to our earlier wish for a perfect parent. Bosses and top management are no more perfect than our parents were. They may be the best we have had, but they are not perfect. Letting go of our dependency and indirect strategies means realizing that our bosses are currently giving us everything that they have to give. It is not that our bosses withhold from us, it is just that in managing the melodrama of their own careers, they have little more to offer us than what they have already bestowed. It was the same with our parents or guardians; they gave us all the love, protection, and control that they had to give. As parents ourselves we come to realize that we give our children all that we have to give and it is still not enough. Robert Hoffman and the people at the Quadrinity Center in San Francisco have identified three stages we have to go through to let go of our parents and claim our autonomy. I think these steps apply equally to freeing us from being overly focused on the behavior of people above us in our own work hierarchy.

1. Disappointment. We first acknowledge that we are disappointed that we are not getting more support, honesty, direction, or freedom from those above us. We have to face the fact that we are not getting what we need and that we may never get it.

2. Anger. We have to acknowledge the anger we feel because those above us are not giving us what we want. When they took the job of boss, they also took on an obligation to serve those who work for them. They are in some ways not fulfilling that obligation, and we resent it. Some of us tend to bury the resentment we feel toward those above us. The fear is that if we owned up to the resentment, it would be an act of disloyalty and get us in trouble. This step is to say, even to ourselves, that we are not only disappointed, but we are angry that our management is not all that we wish it to be.

3. Compassion. After the hard feelings have become clear, the final step is to forgive. Forgive ourselves for having tried so hard to please with only moderate success. We also feel compassion for our bosses for being caught between trying to be good supervisors and eagerly striving to please those above them. What is hard to accept as a subordinate is that most of our bosses' attention is aimed upward. They want corner offices just like we do. We need to forgive them for their ambition and for being not much better than we are. It is hard for us to feel compassion for people in power. Just because we feel compassion for our bosses does not mean we have to give in to them. In fact, the opposite occurs. Seeing people in power realistically and accepting that they have given us everything they have to give allows us to stop watching them so closely and to get on with the business of operating our own activities in a way that we believe in.

Working through our own attachment with those above us, whether it is through steps like these or some other process (middle age helps), releases us to pursue our enlightened self-interest without distraction. It entails putting some of our "ambition" on a back burner and taking real responsibility for the progress of our function.

If we stop seeking approval, recognition, and safety from our boss, then what should the basis for our relationship with our boss be? We are really partners in making our function successful. Our boss is the senior partner and relates to us somewhat like a banker or a board member would if we truly had our own business.

BOSS AS BANKER.   When bankers make a decision to loan us money, they are looking at four things:

- Clarity about what business we are in. Our boss makes sure we know what business we are in. Our boss helps set the limits of our domain and keeps us focused on what we are here to do.

- Financial accountability. Our boss approves our budget and gets monthly or quarterly reports to ensure that we are living up to the numbers and staying healthy.

- Existence and credibility of users. Our banker and our boss want to know who our customers are. Are they viable customers? Our boss wants to make sure we are serving the right people.

- Quality of our product/service and how we are delivering it. Our boss wants to be sure that our output meets the standards of the larger organization and that we are meeting our commitments.

Other than looking at these four things, bankers/bosses leave us alone. They are available for help if we need them, but how we operate our business is basically up to us. One of the key things bankers/bosses can do for us is help us get resources from the rest of the organization that we cannot get on our own.

BOSS AS BOARD MEMBER. Board members have concerns in addition to those of bankers:

- Board members get involved with us in determining major goals and the direction the unit will take. Before we change the game in any significant way, we need our boss on our side.

- Personnel selection. In addition to declaring dividends, the board member/boss has a legal responsibility to select the president, in this case, us. It is reasonable to have our boss approve key personnel moves. This includes involvement in performance evaluations and succession planning.

- Major promises. Our board member/boss wants to be involved in major goal setting and what results we promise. All of these functions of a boss give bosses a role in planning and ultimate accountability but leave us free to manage our unit in the way we see fit. The entrepreneurial mind-set is that we need a boss for the above things but that we will proceed day to day as if our unit is our own. The vision of greatness for the unit is our own creation and we need no one's permission to act it out. If bosses give us a lot of noise in the process—well, they are doing the best they can; nobody's perfect. If they threaten us with a rotational assignment in Siberia—well, we are all going to peak out someday, and our time has come ahead of schedule.

SEVEN

FACING ORGANIZATIONAL REALITIES:

CONTINUAL ACTS OF COURAGE

To commit ourselves to a vision of greatness, to live out that vision with allies and adversaries, and to claim our autonomy in the process is no easy task. In almost every case it requires an act of courage. We constantly are confronted with the question "If this is my vision, what courage is required of me at this moment?"

Our wish, always, is to find a safe path. We are willing to be political, but we want to do it in a risk-free way. We want to be an advocate for our function, but we want to do it with the blessing of our bosses and peers. The problem is that the very situations that require political skill are the ones that entail some danger. The routine and predictable parts of our jobs require very little political skill. The fact that we do have a vision of greatness means we have chosen to live on the frontier, and the frontier always entails some danger.

Unfortunately, all the safe paths have been taken. Our search for a way to get what we want that does not require courage takes several forms.

We have a religious belief in rationality and data. If logic and the facts are on our side, we hope they alone will be persuasive. There is a bit of an engineer in all of us that worships facts, laws, rules, equations, and predictability. If you can't measure it, it doesn't exist. We take refuge in the belief that being right—factually correct—is enough. Attempting to influence others via facts, data, and logical argument is our strategy of preference. The safest and most reasonable path for us to take is to make demands on others based on the facts, and this often works.

In truly political situations, however, where people's goals and self-interests are in conflict, facts and logic are not enough. Decisions are made leaving the facts far behind. Doggedly clutching our facts and reason when other forces are at play is a way of looking for safety when none exists.

Imitation is another safe path we travel. If we use common language, adhere to company norms, merge with the culture, and look in every respect like we belong here, we hope we will get the resources we need to get the job done. These efforts to fit in are still not enough and are a form of resistance against having to act with courage to achieve our goals. Imitation is the belief that if we strategically mold our behavior in a way that is to other people's liking, they will give us what we want. We thought we could avoid risk by adapting successfully to the people around us.

A third safe path is simply to follow the rules. We learn the formal and unwritten policies and stay within their bounds. If it looks like we are going to exceed our budget, we will postpone further spending. If personnel says we cannot give more than a 10 percent increase to an employee, then that becomes our limit. If we are supposed to have a budget line approved for a project before we start work, then we won't begin until we get formal approval. Working to rule, as stated earlier, is the bureaucratic form of revenge. It is the choice of safety over making something happen and taking personal responsibility for how we operate. It is a belief that if we follow the rules, there is no way someone else can find fault with us. It offers safety, but in finding shelter, we lose our vision, and another slice of our optimism has disappeared.

We are political in a positive way when we act with autonomy in service of our vision. When we do this in the midst of a culture that seems to reward dependency, we feel like we are betting the farm. The conventional belief is that if we stand up we will be shot. Our choice to move ahead even in the face of the risk we are taking is the act of courage. It requires courage to communicate understanding to our adversaries and to acknowledge the suffering we have caused them. To talk to our bedfellows about the trust that is lacking in our relationship is a risk. Admitting to our users that we have made a mistake, telling the organization that we made a promise that we cannot deliver, confronting undue aggressiveness and passivity on the part of our subordinates, giving up some control of territory that traditionally was ours, communicating to management that its own behavior is part of the problem all entail risky business. If our primary goal is to move up the organization, then in most cases we will act with caution. If, however, our primary commitment is to contribute, be of service to our users, treat people well, and maintain our integrity, then we are doomed to a course of adventure, uncertainty, and risk. In fact the very obstacles we fear are there to help us discover our own integrity. Only when we push hard against others and they resist do we really know where we stand. The way that we know we are choosing the right path is that the tide is high and the undertow is strong. If we have found a way of doing our job that does not entail any risk, then the organization probably does not need us. A vision is a preferred future, and acts of courage in the creation of that future give meaning to our work.

There is one type of courage that we don't want. Sometimes people use courage as an excuse for aggression. A manager will use condemning and judgmental language in arguing an issue. This person will publicly condemn other groups and individuals. Public acts of rebellion are not the kind of courage we need. A mutiny or armed revolution does not serve anyone's vision. Part of our vision is a statement of how we want people to treat each other. I have never heard a vision of how people should be treated that argued for violence or attack. We are political when we act as living examples of our vision, and if our vision calls for compassion, we have to act that way. Angry, hostile behavior violates our vision and in that way does not serve the organization. Stating that our aggression was really an act of courage is no excuse. Risks are required, but only as they serve our vision and the people around us.

NONSUICIDAL COURAGEOUS ACTS

The goal is to take reasonable risks, not to commit suicide. Whenever we talk about courage, our minds turn to fantasies of either homicide or suicide. We have grown up with such warlike, dominating, mountain man models of courage that we need a way of being courageous that serves us mere mortals. After all, all we are fighting is bureaucracy; we are not reclaiming the Northwest Territory for our homeland. There are three acts of courage that fit our intent of service and compassion.

ACT ONE: FACING THE HARSH REALITY

It is difficult to take a cold and dispassionate look at our current predicament. Our instinct is to make the best of it and to rationalize any frustration we have. If our goal is to meet all customer requirements, we can easily rationalize falling short. We can adopt the belief that time will make things better. We tend to keep on doing what we are currently doing, and perhaps do more of it.

A product manager was brought into a company that makes automated control devices in order to develop line extensions that would more effectively compete with the Japanese. After analyzing the situation for about six months, he concluded that some radical departures were required. The time between the creation of an idea and the operating tolerances of the control device would have to be altered. For the next four months he proposed, justified, defended his proposals. During this period he kept thinking that he had not adequately made his case. He looked for more data, upgraded his mode of presentation, and lobbied intensively with key people in the organization. The response from top management was arms-length interest. The executives said they wanted to support him, but perhaps the timing wasn't just right. His objective was good, but perhaps the task force structure he proposed for implementing the new strategy was not quite right. He was facing into the teeth of a cautious, territorial, bureaucratic response. His response was to keep trying, be persistent, push harder. The harsh reality in this situation was that the manager had been brought into the company to make changes that the company did not have the stomach to support. It seemed more important for the vice presidents of product development and manufacturing to maintain their current way of doing business than to upset a stable network of relationships in order to give their customers more product choice. In their current product line, in effect, customers often had to pay for a set of features that they did not require. For the product manager, Tom, to face up to the harsh reality — namely, that the company was not acting on the commitment made to him when it hired him — took courage.

It is easier to continue along thinking somehow things will change, allowing ourselves to be "managed," than to face our issues squarely. Any change we wish to make, any vision we want to see realized will have a destabilizing effect on those around us. The act of courage is to call it as it is, acting almost indifferent to the consequences it might have for us. If Tom faces up to the reality of the company's ambivalence about changing, it may mean that there is no role for Tom to play. He might have made a mistake in joining the organization. He might be facing two or three years of frustration and minor support. He might create adversaries if he makes his case too loudly. The fear of losing approval, being misplaced, and living in purgatory leads us to rationalize events. Avoiding our harsh realities, we live in a twilight zone. On the surface we remain hopeful; underneath we know there is something wrong. We avoid facing the reality because at least we know the extent of pain the current situation inflicts on us, and we know we can survive. That is why unhappy couples stay together for thirty years. They know, by their experience, how bad it can get, and they know they can live with it. They are not happy, but they also are not on the street. Better to live with a known amount of suffering than to face the possibility that things can get worse.

The first act of courage, then, is simply to see things as they are. No excuses, no explanations, no illusions of wishful progress. For Tom it is the realization that (1) he is asking the company to make dramatic changes both in the way new products are developed and in its product profile strategy and (2) two key vice presidents are not supporting his proposals and really want a low-risk, pain-free way of becoming more competitive.

Facing the harsh reality has several benefits:

- It allows us to stop wasting energy on adapting, compromising, positioning ways of coping.

- It helps us feel less crazy. Instead of pressuring ourselves to do better, we realize there is something going on here that is deeper and not all our responsibility.

- It strengthens us. Facing reality, acting with courage is a way of reclaiming our autonomy. We know at such moments that our survival is in our own hands, and that is control worth having.

- It enhances our chances of getting support for our projects. Power in an organization is an inside job. When we act in personally powerful ways, we communicate to others a strength that is reassuring to them.

In a way it sounds simple to face up to what is happening. Here are, however, some classic examples in which the courage to face up to the harsh reality was missing.

The core business of a large health care company was gauze and bandages. For years, whenever a new product grew large enough, a new company was created and one of the executives of the original company was made president. The prevailing attitude was that if I can develop a new product line outside of the gauze and bandage line, the organization will soon create a new company and I will be made president. A nice career path for marketing executives. The effect was to neglect and drain the original base business, gauze and bandages. The neglect was hidden by increasing annual sales of the base business. It took a new president to come in and confront the managers with the fact that the parent company was ailing, that the increase in annual sales was strictly due to price increases, that unit sales had in fact been level or decreasing in recent years. He dramatized the plight by declaring that if the number of wounds in the United States didn't increase significantly, the company would be in real trouble. The second harsh reality the new president unearthed was that the executives were too focused on breaking away from the original company to be given their own business. He stated that if they had any careers left at all, it was with the original company. A difficult reality to live with, and it took the courage of a new boss to face it.

A large public power company was years down the road in constructing several nuclear power facilities. Mounting public resistance to nuclear power was being expressed through the state public utilities commission. The PUC was making it harder and harder to get anything up and running. After years of agony the management committee of the nuclear power group faced up to the fact that they could not do the job originally requested of them. They recommended that construction be discontinued and their own organization be scaled down, including the elimination of their own jobs. A tough choice, but the only path that they felt they could honestly recommend.

On a smaller scale, two section heads in an engineering company were struggling with each other over who would come up with the accepted methods for coke particle sizing. (Don't worry if you don't know what coke particle sizing is.) The struggle between them was waged in a rational, logical way for months. Finally a senior engineer had the courage to stand up in a meeting and say, "You two section heads who run these two groups are competing with each other for credit over which group comes up with the sizing method. If the two of you would stop arm wrestling, we could come up with one method and get on with it." A risky statement to make, but good for the business.

ACT TWO: OUR OWN CONTRIBUTION TO THE PROBLEM

We all live with the pervasive wish to proclaim our innocence. Efforts to avoid blame sometimes reach epidemic proportions. As long as it is not our fault, we can live with anything. The beginning of each meeting is spent agreeing that the problems we face are due to forces outside our control and due to people not in this meeting. It all begins early in life. As a child our first complete sentence is "It's not my fault." The curse of being an only child is that there is no one to blame. I have two daughters. More than once I have walked into a room, catching one of my daughters alone with a broken plate lying shattered at her feet.

"What happened Jennifer?" I ask.
"I didn't do it," she answers.
"Who did it?" I ask, getting edgy.
"Heather did it."
"Where is Heather?"
"I don't know."
"Heather isn't home now."
"Well somehow the plate fell on the floor."

"It wasn't my fault." And so it goes, on and on for years.

At work the pattern continues. Problems we face are typically caused elsewhere. It is easy to blame others. It takes courage to hold ourselves responsible for the difficulties we face. It is rare and shocking to hear someone say, "I missed the schedule because I did not manage the project well." Blame avoidance is the essence of the bureaucratic mind-set. Feeling personally responsible is the essence of the entrepreneurial mind-set. To be a bureaucrat is to experience ourself as a victim. It takes strength and courage to acknowledge that the success and failure of our project, our function, our business, in fact our lives, is our own creation. Sometimes in the abstract we are able to admit that we are basically responsible for our lives, but in the concrete specifics of this moment, it is rarely our fault.

What is required to be a living example of our vision is to own up to our contribution to the problem. It is not that, in fact, we are the only cause of our problem. Other people and groups and external forces do strongly impact upon us. There is evil in the world. Some people are out to get us and do hurt us. Sometimes our bosses are making decisions that make it impossible to do our jobs well. It is just that we cannot control anything other than our own actions. We can make demands on others, we can give them orders, but ultimately they control themselves and we control ourselves. For this reason when we blame others, we render ourselves helpless. We personally cannot fix a problem that we have not helped to create. So while it is not totally accurate to only focus on our contribution to the problem, it is the most functional thing to do. Having the courage to see the part of a problem that we have created, that it is our rake we have stepped on, empowers us to take action to fix it.

The trick is to own up to our own responsibility without allowing the inevitable guilt we feel to immobilize us. There is no way around the guilt, and in fact the guilt simply means that we have made a choice. We can avoid guilt only by not choosing. Standing still, not moving, watching the world go by. As managers we have power over other people's lives. We do things that hurt other people's lives, and we cannot totally justify this or explain it away. We live with a certain amount of guilt; it is OK, and we will pile up some more before it is over.

Sometimes when I ask people what their contribution to the problem is, they respond by identifying their contribution to the solution. They say, "I tried this and this and this." No. No. That is what you did to try and help the situation. The question is what have you done to get in the way? I then get a surprised expression, hands thrown up in the air, and the cry, "Me?"

Because we live in bureaucracies that encourage caution, people's contribution to the problem is usually a sin of omission. It is most often what we did not do that gets us in trouble. When elderly people are asked what they regret about their lives, it is most often those things that they did *not* do. The same with us in organizations. We have chosen not to confront a problem. We hope that time will heal all wounds. We are reluctant to upset people by bringing skeletons out of the closet, we use compassion as an excuse to postpone, and we believe that the messenger will be shot.

When we define a preferred future, we commit to live now according to that vision and do that most dramatically when we take responsibility for what is happening around us. This is particularly true for members of top management. When they articulate their core values or culture, they need to make sure they themselves are acting in accordance with those values. Their most powerful act is to examine what they are doing that gets in the way of the values being expressed. If it happens at this level it lays the groundwork for others down the organization to truly have courage and take responsibility for the success of the business.

ACT THREE: AUTHENTIC STATEMENT IN THE FACE OF DISAPPROVAL

The third act of courage is to say what needs to be said to those who need to hear it. Being authentic is putting into words what we see happening. An important part of being authentic is expressing the first two elements of courage: the harsh reality facing us, and our own contribution to the problem. Often people feel that to be authentic in this way is to be suicidal. They claim other people don't want to hear bad news (the harsh reality) and why add insult to injury by announcing that there is not only bad news, but they are partly to blame for it. This fear of others' disapproval starts the whole bureaucratic cycle. It is true that no one really likes to hear bad news; when we do hear it, our first question is who is at fault. But the fact that we have raised the tension level and put ourselves in an awkward situation is no excuse not to go ahead with our authentic statements. At such moments we have to choose between what may be good for our career (innocence and silence) and what may be good for the organization. Being authentic even in the face of disapproval is at any time the unique contribution we have to make. It does go against the culture, because most cultures are engaged in role playing, looking good, disguising problems — all variations on running for office. Being authentic is a risk worth taking and does require courage.

The fear of being direct often is our own creation. Our caution in making direct statements hurts us much more than other people's resentment at what we have to say. It is easier to hear bad news than to deliver it. If you are a manager, do you want your people to tell you the truth or not? Most of us answer yes. So why are our own bosses any different than we are? The only difference between us and people at higher levels is that they have more power than we do. Because they have power over us, we tend to distort the intensity and destructiveness of their response. As a result we get very cautious and they get frustrated because no one tells them what is really going on.

The authentic statement names the harsh reality, identifies our part in it, and finally states what we want from others to make things work. The essence of our dialogue with others at work is to exchange our wants. In personal relationships, the essence is to exchange feelings, but at work our most productive meetings are simply "Here is what I want from you. What do you want from me?" Simple conversations using our six-year-olds as role models.

The only time I have seen acts of courage backfire is when they were done with anger. Our vision calls for us to treat others well, so even in stressful moments, we want to treat others and ourselves with compassion. Acts of courage are political and positive because they go against the culture in a way that serves our vision. We are political when we are advocates seeking support for a way of operating, a set of values and beliefs. We are positive in our advocacy when our actions are aligned with those values.

EIGHT

ENACTING THE VISION:

THE ESSENCE OF EMPOWERMENT

The purpose of this chapter is to explain briefly how to move in a direction that supports our own empowerment and to create an environment that supports the empowerment of others. The actions we can take depend in part on how much of the organization we have under our control. If we sit on top of the pyramid we can have a very broad impact on structure, policy, strategy, and procedures. If the pyramid sits on top of us, our direct impact may be confined to our own unit or even our own individual actions, if we are a sole contributor. In a way it doesn't matter where we sit. The challenge is to pursue our vision with as much courage and intensity as we can generate. If we are fortunate, the vision we have is aligned with the broad intentions of those running our organization. We may be a part of one of the sweeping programs that are taking place in many large companies. Even if we are part of a major change effort, though, we are still faced with the individual problem of what we do this afternoon and first thing tomorrow morning. Lasting improvement does not take place by pronouncements or official programs. Change takes place slowly inside each of us and by the choices we think through in quiet wakeful moments lying in bed just before dawn. Culture is changed not so much by carefully planned, dramatic, and visible events as by focusing on our own actions in the small, barely noticed, day-to-day activities of our work. In a way, the only culture that exists for us is in the room in which we are standing at the moment. It is the transformation of the culture of the room we are in that holds the possibility of transforming the culture of the rest of the organization. It is change from the inside out. The meeting I am a part of at this moment is a microcosm of the organization as a whole. It is fairly easy for us to see that the culture of the organization impacts each of our encounters. Our task is to reverse this process: to believe that if we create a unique culture in this meeting, this will in turn act as a backwash and begin to change the culture of the rest of the organization. If we change one part of a system, the whole system is affected. When we each focus on the present and become living examples of the organization we wish to create, the larger change process has begun. This is the essence of positive political acts. It is the political meaning of Ghandi. Choosing to start every day by weaving cloth. This daily act of self-reliance had as much meaning for Indian independence as Ghandi's discussion about political strategy. Being attentive to the integrity of our own actions is the only practical way for most of us to feel that we have some control and choice about the future. Our actions in service of an organization we believe in are the antidote to our feelings of helplessness. Otherwise we are left waiting for others either to follow us or to lead us. We are all getting too old to wait for Rip Van Winkle to wake from his sleep. We become empowered when we create around ourselves a bubble that expresses our wishes of what we want to create. The bubble is the way we and our unit operate. This is the entrepreneurial act.

MOVING TOWARD TENSION

Organizations have a tendency to become institutes for the very, very nervous. To relax at work is usually a contradiction in terms. I heard Soupy Sales on the radio say, "If you want to have a nervous breakdown, you have two choices. You can check yourself into a mental institution or you can go to work for NBC, where nobody will notice." Given the huge investment most of us make in our work plus the competitive environment we operate in, it is only natural that people are constantly bouncing off each other. Our instinctive reaction is to avoid tension and conflict. In our wish to find a safe path it is easy to avoid difficult issues and stay away from people that might give us a hard time.

The act of moving away from tension does not eliminate it; it just postpones it. Our discomfort with tension is our fear that we may lose control if the discussion becomes too intense. I may say things I don't really mean (which is code for worrying about saying things I do really mean). We all know people whose basic life stance is to smooth things over so that it all looks like it is going according to plan. The essence of bureaucracy is never to get excited about anything. It can become more important to maintain peace and quiet waters than to get a problem resolved.

The alternative is to move toward the tension. Tension can be viewed as a sign of life. There is a fine line between anxiety and excitement. The fact that there is tension in the room means that people care about what is happening. When we drain the tension out of a situation, we have to be careful we have not unintentionally dampened commitment. Moving toward tension means beginning a dialogue about the difficult issue facing us. The restraint on us that keeps conflict from being destructive is that in the process of confronting we continue to treat each other as human beings. Better to move toward conflict and run the risk of hurt feelings than to avoid conflict and let the business suffer.

The other reason to move toward tension is that it is a source of learning about oneself. Almost every important learning experience we have ever had has been stressful. Those issues that create stress for us give us clues about the uncooked seeds within us that need our attention. Stress and anxiety are an indication that we are living our lives and making choices. The entrepreneurial approach is to view tension as a vehicle for discovery. Dissatisfied customers teach us how to do business. People who do not use our services teach us how to sell. Other departments that are angry with us teach how to improve our product, service, and way of working with them. Moving toward tension is the belief that the fire of the marketplace tempers and strengthens our ability to survive.

FINAL THOUGHTS

We all have the task of translating our vision into specific steps that fit our situation. Most of all we need to maintain our sense of hope and optimism.

One place to look for hope is within our own experience. For many of us, one of the most positive work experiences has been as part of some kind of start-up operation. Start-ups seem to bring out the best in us — whether they involve project engineers engaged in a plant expansion in Europe, marketing people launching a new brand, or any one of us taking an idea we have had and nurturing it into reality. When we are starting something new, we feel free to create many of our own rules. We create structure and procedures that are totally responsive to the needs of the situation. We join others on the project as equals, regardless of title. We sacrifice comforts, commit long hours, and think about how to make the project work all the time. We are also willing to take risks that normally we wouldn't take. Communication tends to be very direct, with our concern for the project outweighing our concern for people's sensitivities. Start-ups are stressful, hard on our family life, and exciting. Part of what makes them productive is that we know they are only temporary and so the normal bureaucratic way of operating is suspended. We haven't got time or energy to be political or manipulative with each other.

Many organizations have realized that their normal bureaucratic ways have to be set aside to encourage any entrepreneurial effort. Special new ventures groups, business teams, "skunkworks," task forces, even compensation systems, are created to get around the normal way of doing business.

Our own experience with start-up efforts gives us clues about how to create within our current unit an organization we believe in. We want to create conditions in our normal way of doing business that typically have only existed in temporary, countercultural efforts such as start-ups. Our goal in a way is to make every unit have some of the qualities of a start-up.

We do this, knowing that we are facing an uphill battle. The tragedy we have seen in the last ten years of successful social experiments is that the parent company or larger organization has been so slow to learn. We create or allow a pocket of entrepreneurial effort, and then as it becomes more and more successful, we try to force it to conform to the bureaucratic system of the larger body. The same thing happens with many acquisitions. We buy a successful small company and then ask it to live by our rules. Something is lost in the process, and most acquisitions forever remain promises unfulfilled.

The answer is not to create more and more protected pockets. It is to recreate the larger institution. This will happen as each employee realizes that the task is his or her own responsibility. We are all looking for hopeful signs that this is taking place.

I am constantly asked, where is this positive politics being put into practice? Has any organization really been able to maintain an entrepreneurial spirit over the years? Where is there an organization that has eliminated the negative political games? Where has a commitment been made and achieved to create an authentic organization? We want proof and evidence. Behind the questions is our fear that these concepts about vision, greatness, courage are not practical and won't work in the real world.

The only honest answer to these questions is that we, in fact, don't know what is possible. We can point to hopeful examples.

- A chairman of the board of Levi Strauss who has articulated a vision for the business and indeed made a personal commitment that members of his management committee will themselves live that vision.

- Ford Motor Company selecting 325 people to do nothing but help make its employee involvement process a reality. Major divisions in Ford deciding that they are going to treat their own people and their customers as number one—and mean it.

- A company within a health care conglomerate that has instituted practices that truly support an entrepreneurial spirit. This is a company that is eliminating secrecy, large status differences, and other trappings of bureaucracy and instituting reward systems and decision-making practices that put commitment to contribution to the organization first and individual career concerns second or third.

- Every company I come in contact with has some kind of social experiment taking place. Some are creating a statement of common values; others are identifying the entrepreneurial pockets of protection. Quality programs abound, usually with a strong component of employee involvement as their cornerstone. Data about what is working elsewhere, unfortunately still don't answer our question of what is possible or practical. The question is very personal. What is truly relevant is what is possible in our own situation and no one else can answer that for us. Our wish for external evidence is another expression of our wish for safety. There is no safe way to create an organization of our own choosing. Even if we had irrefutable evidence that Ford Motor was absolutely successful in its transformation efforts, it wouldn't be data we could rely on. We choose greatness knowing it may never be realized in our lifetime. We all know that even the "excellent" companies in Peters and Waterman's *In Search of Excellence* really aren't as magical as they are described. 3M has segments that are entrepreneurial and segments that are bureaucratic and like an old lady. The same with Disney, McDonald's, and IBM. Parts of these companies lack pride, motivation, and a commitment to the customer. But so what.

We commit ourselves to operate in a way that we believe in because it is what we have to do. Other people's experience may act as signposts for us, but we take the trip alone. It is the task of each of us to build a unit that other people will write about. We confront our own doubts and pessimism by acting as if something more were possible. Knowing all along that we may be naive and foolish. The question is "Can you prove to me that what you propose will work?" The answer is no. To the question "If I pursue politics in a positive way, will I be successful?" the answer is that there is no way of knowing— and there is a chance you will fail. Every act of creation is an act of faith. The essence of faith is to proceed without any real evidence that our effort will be rewarded. The act of faith in choosing to live out a way of operating that we alone believe in gives real meaning to our work and our lives.

The Commitment We Make to Ourselves

- We are the architect of the organization, choosing its form and future. We are not just a laborer, following another's plans.

- We set goals that are unique and that no one else has achieved before in the same way.

- We choose the path of high resistance and live with the anxiety that creates.

- We risk all we have. Not for the thrill of it, but because there is no safe path.

- We are the place of last resort. There is no one to take care of us.

- We are responsible for problems; if we don't handle them, no one will.

ANNOTATED BIBLIOGRAPHY

This list is in no way a survey of the literature. It is a list of books that have had special meaning in understanding what is at stake in empowering managers. Following each title is a comment on the focus of the book.

Albran, Kellogg, *The Profit.*   This is a parody of the master-devotee relationship. It puts our wish to find answers outside ourselves in a good perspective. It's also funny.

Allen, Woody, *Getting Even.*   Woody Allen makes the absurd seem natural and normal— a process we, as managers, are constantly trying to accomplish.

Bean, E., Ordowich, C., Wesley, W. A. "Including the Supervisor in Employee Involvement Effort," *National Productivity Review*, Winter 1985–86, pp. 64–77.   Practical, well-written article outlining ways to support the empowerment of the supervisor.

Bennis, W., and Nanus, B., *Leaders.*   A fine book on the loftier aspects of leadership. Very clear on the role the Vision plays in translating intentions into action.

Block, Peter. *Flawless Consulting*.

This book is on how to be more effective as an internal consultant/staff person. It expresses, in another form, the values that underlie *The Empowered Manager*.

Bugental, J.F.T., *The Search for Authenticity*.

A therapeutic perspective toward affirming our own existence. A readable book about the ways we stop ourselves from getting what we want.

Dass, Ram, *Be Here Now*.

A visually and spiritually touching book. This book can help integrate living in the marketplace with our internal and external search for God.

Frankl, Victor E., *Man's Search for Meaning*.

More than anything else I have read, this book offers the hope and belief that we have choice regardless of our external circumstances.

Gallwey, Tim, *The Inner Game*.

A masterful discussion of how to integrate learning, performing, and fun. It is really a book on self-management.

Heller, Joseph, *Something Happened*.

An artist's view toward life in an organization that is disturbingly realistic.

Hoffman, Bob, *Everyone's at Fault, No One Is to Blame*.

Very practical guide to confronting dependency and working through our authority issues.

Koestenbaum, Peter, *Managing Anxiety*.

A wonderful tool for understanding anxiety and the role it plays in our development.

Kopf, Sheldon, *No Hidden Meanings*.

Powerful book of photographs and quotes that touch our deepest fears and longings.

Kopf, Sheldon, *If You Meet the Buddha On the Road, Kill Him*.

A discussion of how our lives are in our own hands and our searches are eternal.

Naisbitt, J., and Aburdene, P., *Reinventing the Corporate Future*.

Reassuring documentation that the changes in organizations many of us hope for are already happening.

Golf Digest, *World's 50 Greatest Golf Courses*.

Just kidding. Sometimes I think if I ever find Greatness it will be on the 18th hole at Pebble Beach.

INDEX